PRAISE FOR ANN REARDON
AND *HOW TO COOK THAT*

"Ann Reardon is one of the sweetest bakers on YouTube. Her experience as a food scientist takes her confections to the next level—they are as creative as they are delicious. You will thoroughly enjoy every mouth-watering page of her first cookbook."

—Rosanna Pansino (Nerdy Nummies)

"Ann Reardon was a food scientist and a dietician before creating her massively popular channel called How to Cook That. Reardon focuses mainly on desserts, including novelty cakes and complicated baking techniques. She also teaches people how to fix baking fails and turn them into beautiful dessert creations."

—*Vogue*

"*How to Cook That* is the most popular Australian cooking channel in all the world, and it's not hard to see why. Any sweet tooth would be entranced by Ann's videos documenting her creations, which cover all things dessert, from cake to chocolate."

—Popsugar

"Ann Reardon is a food scientist, which is sort of like being a chef who knows not only how to cook but why the things you're doing in the kitchen happen the way they do."

—The Blemish

"Australia's Queen of Desserts."

—*The Sydney Morning Herald*

CRAZY SWEET
CREATIONS

ANN REARDON

Coral Gables

FOR MY WONDERFUL BOYS,
JAMES, MATTHEW & JEDD.

CONTENTS

INTRODUCTION

The top shelf of my studio pantry is just for chocolate! The one below has containers brimming with sweet confections, then there's a range of flours, sugars, cocoa powder and on the bottom shelf... fondant, sprinkles, edible gold and gel food colors for cake decorating.

This may all seem rather strange for a dietician! But I always remember my university lecturer's advice: if you're going to have chocolate, then make sure it's only a small amount and top quality, rather than lots of cheap junk. In other words, you can still enjoy good health without completely sacrificing dessert. But because you can only have a small amount, ensure that your occasional sweet treat is truly delicious!

That idea set me off on a quest to find the best-tasting desserts, many of which now grace the pages of this book. An unexpected bonus is that I've found beautiful baking also builds a sense of community, as family and friends are always excited to pop over for a slice of my latest sweet creation. (Although in the case of a Giant Ice Cream Sandwich, you'll probably need a party.)

Sweet food and baking have always interested me far more than savory dishes. I think they appeal to my creative side, my sweet tooth, and the food scientist in me. Little changes in baking recipes can have a huge effect on flavor and texture. Some people see that as a difficulty but I see it as a challenge. How much can I bend the rules, tweak the ingredients and experiment to make a better version of the recipe—or create something completely new?

Some time ago, I was looking through my mum's bookshelf and found a two-hundred-year-old cookbook. I gently held this piece of culinary history; its pages were stained with age and the cover was falling apart. I have since made many desserts from that book, including a fruit mince pie with meat in it and strawberry ice cream with bugs! As I began researching old cookbooks and their authors, I found myself inspired to write my own. Yes, I have a website and a YouTube channel with hundreds of episodes, but there is something special about a book—the permanency of print. A website can be hacked, and YouTube may be long gone in two hundred years. But a book—this book—well, I'd love to think that it is a small slice of history to be enjoyed right now, shared with friends and eventually passed on to the next generation.

FUN EASY
DESSERTS

FUN EASY DESSERTS

Whether you're an expert or a beginner in the kitchen, we all need a handful of simple but impressive dishes in our repertoire. These are guaranteed crowd-pleasers; it doesn't require a lot of baking experience to create something lovely.

Over the years, I've come to realize that my recipes are enjoyed by people with a wide range of culinary skills, from qualified chefs to mums, dads, and eager children who often send pictures of their amazing cakes and desserts.

I believe that baking should be accessible and enjoyed by all. So if you are a beginner then this chapter is a good place to start. Perhaps next, you can go through and choose to make just one element of a more complex dessert, like the chocolate mousse in the spiral chocolate caramel domes (page 58) or the caramel sauce in the melting chocolate 'n' peanut ball (page 62).

Don't give up if you make a mistake. As Thomas Edison once said of his long journey to inventing the light bulb, we don't fail, we just learn one more way not to do it. I've certainly learnt plenty of ways **not** to do things. I have seized chocolate, burnt caramel, and forgotten to add baking powder to a cake. I have messed up my microwave and smoked out my kitchen, and I've even watched sadly as I defrosted an elaborate 3D cake and the fondant slowly "melted" before my eyes. (My takeaway lesson from that occasion: don't freeze fondant covered cakes!) Just keep trying and you'll become a better baker for it.

MINT OREO MOUSSE

A delightful dessert served in mini ceramic plant pots, creating a fresh and fun garden vibe. Dig in, literally, and enjoy the mint chocolate Oreo mousse below the Oreo "soil."

Makes 6.

MOUSSE

12 Oreos (133 g / 4.7 oz)
1 ⅔ cups (400 mL / 13.5 fl oz) heavy cream (35 percent fat)
A few drops of peppermint essence

DECORATION

6 Oreos (65 g / 2.3 oz)
6 sprigs of mint

MOUSSE

Place the Oreos and cream into a bowl, ensuring the cookies are completely covered. Seal the bowl with plastic wrap and refrigerate for at least 3 hours. Using an electric mixer, whip on high speed to form a thick mousse. Stir in the peppermint essence and spoon the mousse into 6 small serving dishes, flattening the top of each one.

DECORATION

Place the Oreos into a Ziploc bag and crush them using a rolling pin until the powder resembles soil. (Don't remove the Oreo filling beforehand as it helps make a moist soil texture.) You can use a food processor for this step if you prefer.

Top each mousse with crushed Oreos and add a sprig of mint to the center of each just before serving.

Video tutorial for this recipe can be found at howtocookthat.net/cookbook

RED VELVET CAKE SHAKE

After a shaky start, Aussie-born Freakshakes have now taken the world by storm! The brainchild of Anna Petridis of Café Patissez in Canberra, these over-the-top shakes were very nearly cut from the menu after the café sold only one in their first month. Thankfully, someone shared their shake online and the rest is history. In the following months, extreme shakes went viral on social media, attracting long queues of eager customers. I filmed an episode about the trend and shared recipes for my own versions of extreme shakes. Since then, bigger and even more extravagant shakes have popped up in cafes all around the globe, from Mumbai to New York.

Makes 1 shake which serves 2 people.

CHOCOLATE BUTTERCREAM

2 tablespoons (22 g / 0.8 oz) margarine or butter

2 tablespoons (12 g / 0.4 oz) cocoa powder

⅓ cup (40 g / 1.4 oz) icing sugar or powdered sugar

MILK CHOCOLATE GANACHE

1 tablespoon (15 g / 0.6 oz) heavy cream (35 percent fat)

1.7 oz (50 g) milk chocolate

WHIPPED CREAM

⅓ cup (75 mL / 2.5 fl oz) heavy cream (35 percent fat)

½ teaspoon vanilla

RED VELVET CAKE

1 slice of red velvet cake (see page 34)

DECORATION AND ASSEMBLY

1 (300 mL / 10 fl oz) weizen beer glass

20 Hershey's kisses

20 red M&Ms

1 scoop of ice cream

2 straws

MILKSHAKE

1 scoop vanilla ice cream

3 tablespoons ganache

1 ¼ cup (300 mL / 10.14 fl oz) milk

CHOCOLATE BUTTERCREAM

Mix together 2 tablespoons cocoa powder, 2 tablespoons butter, and ⅓ cup icing sugar. Using a spatula, squash the butter against the side of the bowl, forcing it to combine with the icing sugar and cocoa. Do not add any liquid.

MILK CHOCOLATE GANACHE

Break the chocolate into pieces and place into a bowl. Add the cream on top and microwave on high for 30 seconds. Stir well and if there are still lumps, microwave for 10 seconds more, then stir until smooth. Leave the bowl at room temperature until you are ready to use the ganache. If it is too thick when you need it, microwave for 5 seconds and stir.

WHIPPED CREAM

Place the cream and vanilla into a bowl and whip until it forms peaks and will hold its shape. Place into a piping bag.

MILKSHAKE

Place the ice cream, ganache and milk into a blender and mix until smooth.

DECORATION AND ASSEMBLY

Spread chocolate buttercream around the outside of the top of the glass. Press Hershey's kisses and M&Ms into the buttercream. At this point you can store the glass in the fridge until you are ready to use it.

Pour milkshake into the glass to about two thirds full. Add a scoop of ice cream. Pipe whipped cream on top of the ice cream. Add the straws and a slice of red velvet cake to top it off. Serve immediately.

Video tutorial for this recipe can be found at howtocookthat.net/cookbook

COOKIES & CREAM EXTREME SHAKE

Makes 1 shake which serves 2 people and 16 cookies.

CHOC-CHIP COOKIES
(makes 16 large cookies)

1 cup (250 g / 8.8 oz) margarine or butter

2 cups (462 g / 16.3 oz) (firmly packed) brown sugar

2 teaspoons vanilla

2 eggs (100 g / 3.5 oz)

3 cups (480 g / 16.9 oz) plain or all-purpose flour

1 teaspoon baking powder

2 cups (156 g / 5.5 oz) desiccated coconut

8.8 oz (250 g) milk chocolate chips

2.8 oz (80 g) chocolate chips

WHITE CHOCOLATE GANACHE

1 tablespoon (15 g / 0.6 oz) heavy cream (35 percent fat)

1.7 oz (50 g) white chocolate

MILK CHOCOLATE GANACHE

1 tablespoon (15 g / 0.6 oz) heavy cream (35 percent fat)

1.7 oz (50 g) milk chocolate

WHIPPED CREAM

⅓ cup (75 mL / 2.5 fl oz) heavy cream (35 percent fat)

½ teaspoon vanilla

MILKSHAKE

1 scoop vanilla ice cream

1 teaspoon vanilla

1 ¼ cups (300 mL / 10.1 fl oz) milk

DECORATION & ASSEMBLY

1 (300 mL / 10 fl oz) weizen beer glass

½ chocolate chip cookie, crushed

0.35 oz (10 g) chocolate chips

2 scoops of ice cream

2 cookies

1 extra scoop vanilla ice cream

0.7 oz (20 g) melted chocolate to drizzle

2 straws

CHOC-CHIP COOKIES

Preheat the oven to 180°C (350°F).

Place the butter, sugar and vanilla into a mixing bowl and beat until light and fluffy. Add the eggs and beat well. Stir in the flour, baking powder, coconut, and chocolate chips. Take 3 tablespoons of mixture and place onto a lined baking tray. Use your hand to flatten each and shape into a round cookie. Repeat with the rest of the mixture. Bake for 15 minutes or until golden. As soon as they come out of the oven arrange the extra chocolate chips on the top of the cookies. Allow to cool before using.

WHITE CHOCOLATE GANACHE

Break the chocolate into pieces and place into a bowl. Add the cream on top and microwave on high for 30 seconds. Stir well and, if there are still lumps of chocolate in the ganache, microwave for 10 seconds more and stir until smooth. Place the bowl in the freezer for 1 hour to thicken.

MILK CHOCOLATE GANACHE

See directions on page 16.

WHIPPED CREAM

Place the cream and vanilla into a bowl and whip until it forms peaks and holds its shape. Place into a piping bag.

MILKSHAKE

Put the ice cream, vanilla and milk into a blender and blend together.

DECORATION & ASSEMBLY

Spread the white chocolate ganache around the outside of the top of each glass. Roll the glass in the crushed chocolate chip cookies so that the crumbs stick to the ganache. Add additional chocolate chips to make it look good. Pipe the milk chocolate ganache in drizzles down the inside of the glass. Pour your milkshake into the glass to around two thirds full. Top with two scoops of ice cream. Pipe a swirl of cream on top.

Take another scoop of ice cream and sandwich between two cookies. Carefully place upright on top of the cream, then drizzle with melted chocolate, add two straws on one side, and serve immediately.

Video tutorial for this recipe can be found at howtocookthat.net/cookbook

PEANUT BUTTER PRETZEL OTT SHAKE

Makes 1 shake which serves 2 people.

CHOCOLATE BUTTERCREAM

2 tablespoons (22 g / 0.8 oz) margarine or butter

2 tablespoons (12 g / 0.4 oz) cocoa powder

⅓ cup (40 g / 1.4 oz) icing sugar or powdered sugar

WHIPPED CREAM

⅓ cup (75 mL / 2.5 fl oz) heavy cream (35 percent fat)

½ teaspoon vanilla

MILKSHAKE

1 scoop vanilla ice cream

1 ¼ cups (300 mL / 10.14 fl oz) milk

1 teaspoon vanilla

DECORATION AND ASSEMBLY

1 (300 mL / 10 fl oz) weizen beer glass

1 3-inch (8 cm) pretzel

0.7 oz (20 g) compound chocolate, melted

1 ½ tablespoons (15 g / 0.5 oz) mini M&Ms

2 tablespoons crunchy peanut butter

10 mini Reese's peanut butter cups

24 M&Ms

1 scoop of ice cream

1 pretzel stick

0.7 oz (20 g) chocolate, melted

1.1 oz (30 g) peanut brittle

2 straws

CHOCOLATE BUTTERCREAM

Mix all the ingredients together. Use a spatula to press the butter against the side of the bowl, forcing it to combine with the icing sugar and cocoa. Do not add any liquid.

WHIPPED CREAM

Place the cream and vanilla into a bowl and whip until it forms peaks and will hold its shape. Place into a piping bag.

MILKSHAKE

Place the ice cream, vanilla, and milk into a blender and mix until smooth.

DECORATION AND ASSEMBLY

Pipe the melted chocolate in a zigzag across a large pretzel and sprinkle it with mini M&Ms. Put it to one side to set.

Spread salted peanut butter around the outside top of the glass coming down about an inch. Then spread about an inch of chocolate buttercream below the peanut butter. Press mini Reese's peanut butter cups and M&Ms into the peanut butter and buttercream. Store the glass in the fridge until you're ready to fill it.

Fill to two thirds with milkshake, add a scoop of ice cream, and pipe cream on top. Add a pretzel stick and a couple of straws to one side. Place the M&M coated pretzel on top, poke in some chunks of peanut brittle, and, using a piping bag, drizzle melted chocolate over the top. Serve immediately.

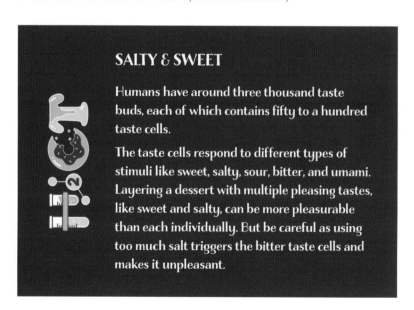

SALTY & SWEET

Humans have around three thousand taste buds, each of which contains fifty to a hundred taste cells.

The taste cells respond to different types of stimuli like sweet, salty, sour, bitter, and umami. Layering a dessert with multiple pleasing tastes, like sweet and salty, can be more pleasurable than each individually. But be careful as using too much salt triggers the bitter taste cells and makes it unpleasant.

Video tutorial for this recipe can be found at howtocookthat.net/cookbook

SPEEDY APPLE TURNOVERS

I love the crunchy layers of puff pastry with the soft warm apple filling served with creamy custard. If you haven't tried making these before, you will be blown away by how simple they are. These apple turnovers are perfect for a winter's night at home with the family, or make extra and serve them up at a large gathering.

Makes 24 turnovers.

6 square sheets of store-bought
    puff pastry
3 ½ cups (800 g / 28.2 oz) tinned
    (canned) unsweetened pie apple
    (or unsweetened apple pie filling)
1 tablespoon (13 g / 0.5 oz) sugar
1 teaspoon cinnamon
Ice cream, cream or custard to serve

Preheat oven to 200°C (390°F).

Mix the apple, sugar, and cinnamon together in a bowl. You can adjust the amount of sugar according to your taste.

Cut each pastry sheet diagonally into quarters to make four triangles. Place a spoonful of apple to one side of each triangle. Fold the triangle in half and use a fork to press and seal along the edges. Bake for 15-20 minutes until crisp and golden. Serve hot with vanilla ice cream, whipped cream, or custard.

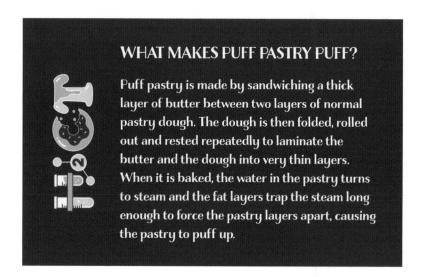

WHAT MAKES PUFF PASTRY PUFF?

Puff pastry is made by sandwiching a thick layer of butter between two layers of normal pastry dough. The dough is then folded, rolled out and rested repeatedly to laminate the butter and the dough into very thin layers. When it is baked, the water in the pastry turns to steam and the fat layers trap the steam long enough to force the pastry layers apart, causing the pastry to puff up.

Video tutorial for this recipe can be found at howtocookthat.net/cookbook

WATERMELON PIZZA

This dessert is perfect in the summer months when watermelon and berries are at their sweetest. The secret is to keep it simple and allow the watermelon to shine as the hero of this recipe.

Makes 4.

1 watermelon (whole)

½ cup (125 g / 4.4 oz) cream cheese

1 tablespoon icing sugar or powdered sugar

1 teaspoon vanilla

⅓ cup (100 g / 3.5 oz) blueberries

2 tablespoons (20 g / 0.7 oz) pistachios, shelled and chopped

⅓ cup (100 g / 3.5 oz) strawberries

Cut a large round slice of watermelon from the center of the melon and remove the rind. You could use a cake ring for a perfect circle.

Mix together the cream cheese, icing sugar and vanilla in a bowl. Spread the cream cheese mixture over the watermelon, leaving a border uncovered around the edge. Wash the strawberries and blueberries and dry with a paper towel. Hull and chop the strawberries. Sprinkle the blueberries, pistachios and strawberries on top of the cream cheese. Cut into pizza shaped slices and serve. This dessert is best made fresh but can be stored in the fridge for several hours.

Video tutorial for this recipe can be found at howtocookthat.net/cookbook

PERFECT
CAKES AND
CUPCAKES

PERFECT CAKES AND CUPCAKES

There are three factors to consider when judging a cake. The first is flavor; it simply has to taste good. Texture is, however, equally important. A rubbery, dense, oily, or excessively dry cake will not be eaten even if it tastes good. The final factor is outward appearance; a cake should have a uniform shape, a crack-free surface, a lightly browned appearance, and be free from stickiness.

The ingredients in a cake all interact to create its unique taste, texture, and appearance. It's not magic, there's actually a lot of science to it all. Unfortunately, the cake recipes that rank highest on outward appearance often do not match up for taste and texture. To me, it's what is on the inside that matters most, so it has to score high on taste and texture to be included in this book.

The following experiments are variations on my perfect vanilla cupcake recipe on page 36. It's important to remember that decreasing the amount of an ingredient will decrease the overall amount of cake batter that is made. For these experiments, an equal weight of cake batter was put into each cup in a cupcake pan to allow for easy comparison.

AMOUNT OF FAT

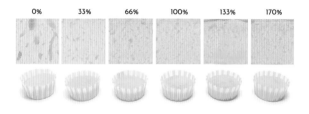

The amount of fat in a cake makes a huge difference to the texture. Not enough fat and the cake will be rubbery and chewy with big uneven air pockets. A good fat level will give small even air pockets and a velvety soft texture. With too much fat, it becomes denser and noticeably greasy in taste.

TYPE OF FAT

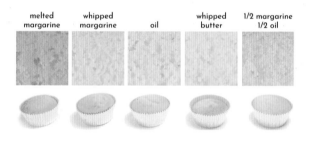

The type of fat used affects both the flavor and the volume or lightness of the cake. Oil makes the lightest, airiest, prettiest cakes, but in this particular recipe, using oil also left an unpleasant taste. Oil can be useful in smaller quantities or if there are other stronger flavors present in the cake.

Butter gives a distinct flavor that some people like and others do not. Margarine generally has a mellower flavor profile, so it is not as detectable in a cake and is my first choice. Whipping the margarine or butter with sugar gives small, even air pockets and a soft pleasant texture. Butter makes a slightly denser cake.

Melting the margarine instead of whipping it results in slightly more uneven air pockets. You can see this when the cake is cut, but it is nearly undetectable when eating it.

AMOUNT OF SUGAR

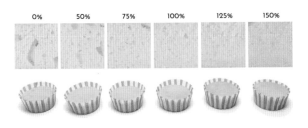

I'm constantly asked by bakers whether they can decrease the amount of sugar in a recipe. Most people know that this will alter the taste, but don't realize it also has a dramatic effect on texture. Using no sugar at all will create large, uneven, air pockets and a denser cake. If you add more sugar than normal, the cake will have a higher volume for the same weight of batter, but it will be crumbly, taste surprisingly eggy, and come out sticky on top.

Just the right amount of sugar results in small, even air pockets and a moist, yummy cake. There is a little bit of wiggle room, though, and trimming back to 75 percent of the sugar will still make an acceptable cake.

AMOUNT OF WATER

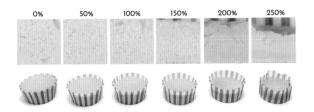

This illustrates perfectly that good outward appearance doesn't always mean the best cake. Using no water produces the best-looking cupcake with the highest volume. But when eaten it will be dry with a metallic baking powder aftertaste. The identical amount of baking powder was undetectable in other cakes with liquid added. In my experiments, I found halving the amount of liquid in a cupcake recipe also looked good, but the full amount created a more moist and delicious cake to eat.

At the other end of the scale, add too much water and your cake will shrivel and turn into a dense, rubbery, egg-flavored mess—hardly a party pleaser!

EGG VARIATIONS

Eggs provide structure and richness to a cake. Simply cutting out the eggs leads to a cake that looks pale and has a paste-like texture, similar to cookie dough. The standard amount of eggs yields a cake with an even, fine crumb.

Doubling the quantity of eggs makes large air pockets and a rubbery texture. This is to be expected because eggs are 75 percent water, so the result is similar to adding too much liquid. So if you wish to add more eggs to your cake, you'll need to decrease another liquid in the recipe.

The final three cakes were the best. Using only the egg yolks (in the same weight as whole eggs) gave a good volume and a cake that was nice looking, albeit slightly yellow. A cake with all egg whites (not whipped) resulted in a lower volume than using all yolks, but it was still a pleasant cake. This is useful to know if you have leftover whites or yolks from another recipe.

Using whole eggs and whipping the egg whites increased the cake volume, resulting in a lighter and fluffier texture. The top was slightly domed in the middle, but I'm in favor of the best-tasting vanilla cake over the best-looking.

VANILLA FLAVOR

When flavoring your vanilla cupcakes, always choose vanilla extract as it gives the most pleasant flavor and aroma. In my experiments, vanilla essence was barely noticeable and vanilla paste negatively affected the color of the cake without improving the flavor.

THE BEST CHOCOLATE CAKE

Have you ever been disappointed by a gorgeous looking chocolate cake that turned out to be dry and tasteless? Well then, this is the recipe for you. This is my all-time favorite chocolate cake recipe. It makes a rich moist cake that tastes like chocolate every time.

Makes 24 cupcakes or two 8-inch (20.5 cm) round cakes.

WHIPPED GANACHE FROSTING

21.2 oz (600 g) milk chocolate

¾ cup (200 mL / 6.8 fl oz) heavy cream (35 percent fat)

RICH CHOCOLATE CAKE

7.1 oz (200 g) dark chocolate with 70 percent cocoa

1 ⅓ cups (315 g / 11.1 oz) margarine or butter

8 large eggs (360 g / 12.7 oz)

2 ¼ cups (485 g / 17.1 oz) caster sugar or superfine sugar

1 ¼ cups (200 g / 7 oz) plain or all-purpose flour

¼ cup (30 g / 1.1 oz) cocoa powder

1 ½ teaspoons baking powder

ASSEMBLY

3.5 oz (100 g) milk or dark chocolate

WHIPPED GANACHE FROSTING

Break the chocolate into pieces and place in a bowl. Bring the cream to a boil, then pour it over the chocolate. Leave it to sit for a couple of minutes and then whisk until smooth. Cover your ganache with plastic wrap and put it into the fridge for at least 3 hours to firm up.

Using an electric mixer, whip the firm ganache until it is fluffy and lighter in color. If the ganache is too thick to whip, heat half a cup in the microwave for 10 seconds, then add this warmed ganache back into the bowl.

RICH CHOCOLATE CAKE

Preheat the oven to 180°C (350°F).

Place chocolate and margarine into a bowl and melt in the microwave on high for 1 minute. Stir the mixture, then microwave for another 30 seconds and stir again. Repeat in 30-second bursts, stirring in between each time, until melted. Mix in the sugar. Then add the eggs and whisk well. Sift the flour, cocoa powder, and baking powder together and mix into the cake mixture until just combined.

Pour into two lined 20.5 cm (8 inch) round cake pans. Bake in the oven for 20-25 minutes or until a knife inserted into the center comes out clean. If your cake is looking done on top but is not yet cooked in the middle, place an empty baking sheet on the oven shelf just above it to protect the top from burning.

Cool on a wire rack.

ASSEMBLY

Level the top of both cakes and place one on a plate or cake stand. Place the whipped ganache into a piping bag fitted with an open star-shaped tip. Pipe dollops of ganache neatly around the edge, then continue piping until the center is covered. Add the second cake on top and repeat the piping pattern.

Using a peeler, shave curls of chocolate onto some baking paper. Pile them on top of the cake in the center. If it is a cold day and your chocolate is hard to shave, just microwave the block for 5 seconds and try again.

Video tutorial for this recipe can be found at howtocookthat.net/cookbook

CHERRY RED VELVET CUPCAKES

Red Velvet seemed to be on everyone's lips, so I set myself a tasty challenge on a trip to New York—to hit up every bakery we passed and find out what all the fuss was about. Oh, what a variety...but not all of it good unfortunately! Some bakeries were serving dry, red-colored vanilla cupcakes with buttercream. Thankfully others had a beautiful, unique flavor with rich cream cheese frosting that left me keen to get home and start experimenting. It wasn't easy but finally, after many disappointing experiments with buttermilk, vinegar, and all the normal variations, I decided to try using morello sour cherry juice. It worked, and I was able to recreate the unique New York red velvet flavor that I was chasing.

Makes 12 cupcakes or one 20 cm (8 inch) round cake.

RED VELVET CAKE

23.6 oz (670 g) jar of morello sour cherries

1 cup (150 g / 5.3 oz) plain or all-purpose flour

2 tablespoons (15 g / 0.5 oz) cocoa powder

¾ cup (165 g / 5.8 oz) sugar

¾ teaspoon powdered gelatin

½ teaspoon salt

1½ teaspoons baking powder

¼ cup (60 mL / 2 fl oz) oil

4 egg yolks (60 g / 2.1 oz)

1 tablespoon (15 mL / 0.5 fl oz) red food coloring

4 egg whites (128 g / 4.5 oz)

¼ teaspoon cream of tartar

CREAM CHEESE FROSTING

⅔ cup (165 g / 5.8 oz) block cream cheese

¼ cup (60 g / 2.1 oz) butter

1⅓ cups (165 g / 5.9 oz) icing sugar or powdered sugar

1 teaspoon vanilla

½ cup (132 g / 4.6 oz) mascarpone cheese

RED VELVET CAKE

Preheat the oven to 170°C (335°F).

Drain the juice from the morello cherries and boil it down to 125 mL (4.2 fl oz) or ½ cup to concentrate the flavor. Set aside to cool.

Place the flour, cocoa powder, sugar, gelatin, salt and baking powder into a bowl and whisk together.

Make a well in the center, then add the oil, egg yolks, concentrated morello cherry juice, and red coloring, but do not stir.

In a different bowl, whip the egg whites with the cream of tartar until soft peaks form.

Using the same beaters, mix the egg yolk and flour mixture on low speed until just combined.

Fold the egg whites into the cake batter in three batches.

Fill each cup in a cupcake pan to ¾ full. (Using an ice cream scoop makes this job easy.) Bake for 11 minutes or until they spring back when lightly touched. Cool completely before frosting.

CREAM CHEESE FROSTING

Leave the cream cheese and butter out of the fridge to soften for at least an hour. Place them both into the bowl of an electric mixer and beat until smooth and pale. Add the icing sugar and lemon juice and beat to combine. Gently fold in the mascarpone.

ASSEMBLY

Take one cupcake and break it into small crumbs. Pipe frosting onto the remaining cupcakes using a star tip, then sprinkle with red velvet crumbs.

Video tutorial for this recipe can be found at howtocookthat.net/cookbook

LEMON MERINGUE CUPCAKES

A beautifully simple affair of vanilla cake filled with lemon curd and topped with luscious Italian meringue frosting. They quickly disappear, leaving you wanting another.

Makes 12 cupcakes.

VANILLA CUPCAKE

⅔ cup (144 g / 5.1 oz) margarine

¾ cup (160 g / 5.6 oz) sugar

4 eggs (180 g / 6.3 oz), separated

1 cup (160 g / 5.6 oz) plain or
    all-purpose flour, sifted

2 teaspoons baking powder

½ cup (110 mL / 3.7 fl oz) water

2 teaspoons vanilla extract

LEMON CURD

Makes 1 cup of curd

⅔ cup (83 g / 2.9 oz) caster sugar or
    superfine sugar

1 egg (45 g / 1.6 oz)

1 egg yolk (15 g / 0.5 oz)

Zest of 1 lemon

½ cup (125 mL / 4 fl oz) fresh lemon
    juice

¼ cup (45 g / 1.6 oz) unsalted butter

ITALIAN MERINGUE RECIPE

3 egg whites (90 g / 3.2 oz)

¼ teaspoon cream of tartar

1 cup (215 g / 7.6 oz) caster sugar or
    superfine sugar

¼ cup (65 mL / 2.2 fl oz) water

Candy thermometer

MY PERFECT VANILLA CUPCAKES

Preheat the oven to 160°C (325°F).

Using electric beaters, cream the margarine and sugar together until light and fluffy. Add the egg yolks and whisk until combined. Add the flour, baking powder, water, and vanilla, and mix until just combined.

Whip the egg whites until they form soft peaks. Add a third of the egg whites into the cake batter and mix through. Then add the remaining egg whites and fold in using a spatula until you can no longer see any egg whites. Be careful to fold rather than mix or you'll knock all the air out of the batter.

Distribute evenly between 12 cupcake cups in a muffin tin; bake for 15 minutes or until cupcakes are golden brown and spring back when lightly touched.

LEMON CURD

Whisk together the sugar, eggs, yolks, lemon zest, and lemon juice.

Microwave on high in one-minute intervals, whisking after each time, until it thickens.

Stir in the butter; once it is melted, strain lemon curd through a fine sieve. Pour into clean jars or drinking glasses, cover (with plastic wrap if using glasses), and store in the refrigerator.

ITALIAN MERINGUE FROSTING

Whisk the egg whites and cream of tartar until they form soft peaks.

Put the sugar and water in a saucepan and bring to a boil. Wash down the sides of the pan with a wet pastry brush, add a candy thermometer to the side of the pan, and leave unstirred until it reaches 114°C (238°F).

Immediately remove the sugar solution from the heat and, with the beaters running, pour in a thin stream into the egg whites. Continue to whisk on high speed until the outside of the bowl no longer feels hot. This usually takes about 5 minutes. You can speed up the cooling process by putting a bowl of iced water underneath the mixing bowl. It will be thick, smooth, and glossy when it is cool.

ASSEMBLY

Using a teaspoon, scoop a small hole in the center of each cupcake. Fill the hole with lemon curd. Pipe a generous swirl of Italian meringue on top of each one.

LIGHT FLUFFY SPONGE CAKE

I once tested so many sponge recipes that my kids got tired of eating cake! Still not fully satisfied with any of the results, I combined a few of the better ones and tweaked the recipe to come up with something new. This sponge cake is light, fluffy, tall, and beautifully moist.

Makes 2 round 8 inch (25 cm) cakes layered into one cake.

SPONGE CAKE

2 cups (320 g / 11.3 oz) plain or
    all-purpose flour

1 ½ cups (330 g / 11.5 oz) sugar

3 teaspoons baking powder

1 teaspoon salt

1 ½ teaspoons (7.5 g / 0.3 oz)
    powdered gelatin

½ cup (125 mL / 4.2 fl oz) vegetable
    oil

7 egg yolks (105 g / 3.7 oz)

1 cup (250 mL / 8.5 fl oz) cold water

7 egg whites (250 g / 8.9 oz)

½ teaspoon cream of tartar

2 teaspoons vanilla extract

ASSEMBLY

2 cups (250 g / 8.8 oz) strawberries

2 ½ cups (600 mL / 20.3 fl oz) heavy
    cream (35 percent fat)

2 tablespoons icing sugar or
    powdered sugar

1 teaspoon vanilla extract

⅓ cup strawberry jam

SPONGE CAKE

Preheat the oven to 160°C (325°F).

Place your flour, sugar, baking powder, salt, and gelatin into a bowl and whisk it to incorporate air and eliminate any lumps. Make a well in the center and pour in the oil, egg yolks, water and vanilla, but do not mix.

In a separate bowl, whisk together the egg whites and cream of tartar on high speed until they form soft peaks. Using the same beaters, mix together the flour mixture on low speed until it is just combined. Fold in the egg whites in three batches.

Spread the mixture evenly in two lined 20 cm (8 inch) cake pans and bake for 35–45 minutes.

ASSEMBLY

Whip together the cream, icing sugar, and vanilla until it is thick enough to hold its shape. Do not over-whip the cream or the fat and liquid will separate.

Wash and slice the strawberries. Reserving the perfect center slices for the top of the cake, dice the remaining pieces. Spread jam on top of one of the cakes. Then using a large round piping tip (or a Ziploc bag with the corner cut off), pipe round dollops of whipped cream around the edge of the cake, dragging the tail of each one toward the center. Pipe more whipped cream in the center of the cake and cover with diced strawberries, then place the second cake on top. For the top of the cake, pipe whipped cream around the around the edge in the same way, then pipe a second circle of dollops just inside the first. Finish with more whipped cream in the center and lovely strawberry slices between each dollop of whipped cream.

Video tutorial for this recipe can be found at howtocookthat.net/cookbook

WHY USE GELATIN IN A CAKE?

In this recipe both the egg yolks and gelatin act as emulsifiers. Emulsifiers help ingredients that don't normally mix, such as oil and water, to combine.

Using emulsifiers increases batter stability during mixing and baking, resulting in a moister cake with uniform aeration. This is why all boxed cake mixes include emulsifiers.

LEMON & BLUEBERRY CAKE

This recipe was a happy little accident. After experimenting with something completely different that didn't work, I simply threw in a few more ingredients and baked it as a cake. The result was so delicious that it is now one of my go-to recipes.

Makes 24 slices.

LEMON & BLUEBERRY CAKE

2 ⅓ cups (515 g / 18.1 oz) margarine

3 ⅓ cups (415 g / 14.6 oz) icing sugar or powdered sugar

12 eggs (600 g / 21 oz)

5 cups (520 g / 18.3 oz) almond flour

Zest of 2 lemons

4 teaspoons baking powder

1 ¼ cups (180 g / 6.3 oz) plain or all-purpose flour

1 cup (150 g / 5.3 oz) frozen blueberries

LEMON BUTTERCREAM

1 ½ cups (360 g / 12.7 oz) butter or margarine

7 ½ cups (1 kg / 2.2 pounds) icing sugar or powdered sugar

2 tablespoons of lemon juice

ASSEMBLY

1 ⅓ cups (200 g / 7 oz) fresh blueberries

LEMON & BLUEBERRY CAKE

Preheat the oven to 180°C (350°F).

Place the margarine, icing sugar, eggs, almond flour, vanilla extract, and lemon zest into a bowl. Whip until the mixture is smooth and really well combined. Add the flour and baking powder and fold until just combined. Spread evenly into two lined 25 x 38 cm (10 x 15 inch) cake pans and sprinkle with frozen blueberries. Bake for 20-25 minutes. Cool before frosting.

LEMON BUTTERCREAM

Use an electric mixer to whip together the icing sugar and margarine until smooth and fluffy, then add the lemon juice and mix until it is just combined.

ASSEMBLY

Sandwich the two cakes together using buttercream, then spread a layer of buttercream across the top and down the sides of the cake. Place the remaining buttercream in a piping bag and pipe around the top edge. Add fresh blueberries to the top of the cake.

Video tutorial for this recipe can be found at howtocookthat.net/cookbook

ALMOND FLOUR VS. ALMOND MEAL

Almond flour is made from blanched (boiled and peeled), finely ground almonds. Some brands also call this "almond meal." However, other producers make almond meal that is more coarsely ground and is made from almonds that have not been peeled, giving it a brown speckled appearance.

MOIST CARROT CAKE

Carrot cake is my husband's favorite, so this recipe gets baked in all sorts of shapes and sizes for his birthday every year. One year, it was shaped like a bowl of spaghetti, while the next one had a Star Wars theme! My cream cheese frosting is creamier and slightly less sweet than most, and the carrot crispies add an artisan bakery touch... Once you've tried them, you won't make carrot cake without them.

Makes one loaf or 12 cupcakes.

MOIST CARROT CAKE

⅓ cup (100 mL / 3.4 fl oz) vegetable oil

⅔ cup (140 g / 4.9 oz) sugar

2 eggs (90 g / 3.2 oz)

1 cup (140 g / 4.9 oz) crushed pineapple, drained

4 medium (140 g / 4.9 oz) carrots, coarsely grated

1 cup (140 g / 4.9 oz) plain or all-purpose flour

1 ½ teaspoons baking powder

½ teaspoon cinnamon

1 cup (120 g / 4.2 oz) of walnuts, roughly chopped

¾ cup (60 g / 2.1 oz) desiccated coconut

CREAM CHEESE FROSTING

½ cup (125 g / 4.4 oz) block cream cheese

3 tablespoons (45 g / 1.6 oz) butter

1 cup (125 g / 4.4 oz) icing sugar or powdered sugar

⅓ cup (100 g / 3.5 oz) mascarpone

1 teaspoon vanilla or lemon juice

CARROT CRISPIES

⅓ cup (70 g / 2.5 oz) caster sugar or superfine sugar

2 ½ tablespoons (40 mL / 1.35 fl oz) or 2 ½ tablespoons water

⅓ cup (37 g / 1.3 oz) coarsely grated carrot

MOIST CARROT CAKE

Preheat the oven to 180°C (350°F).

Pour the oil, sugar, and eggs into a bowl and mix together using a whisk. Stir in the pineapple and carrots.

Sift in the flour, baking powder, and cinnamon and mix until nearly combined. Add the walnuts and the coconut and mix well.

Bake in a lined 4 x 8 x 3 inch (21 x 10.5 x 7.5 cm) loaf pan for 30–40 minutes or until a knife inserted into the center comes out clean. Cool completely before frosting.

CREAM CHEESE FROSTING

Leave the butter and cream cheese out of the fridge to soften for at least an hour. Using an electric mixer, beat together until smooth and pale. Add the sifted icing sugar and either the vanilla or lemon juice and beat again. Fold in the mascarpone cheese.

Once the cake is completely cooled, slather the top in a thick layer of this gorgeous frosting.

CARROT CRISPIES

Place the sugar and water into a saucepan and stir until the sugar dissolves. Add the carrot and stir briefly until it is coated in the sugar syrup. Wash down the sides of the pan with a wet pastry brush and continue to boil over high heat until the sugar is caramelized.

To check if it is ready, take the pan off the heat and place a small amount of carrot on a sheet of baking paper in the fridge. Once cooled, it should set like sticky toffee. If it is not yet done, return to the heat. Once ready, pour the hot mixture onto baking paper and spread out into bite-sized chunks. Leave to cool completely, then put a line of carrot crispies down the middle of the frosted loaf.

HEART INSIDE CUPCAKES

These little beauties will reveal a heart no matter which side you bite. So whether you're making them for a friend or for someone you hope will become a very good friend, you're guaranteed to get a big smile.

Makes 18 cupcakes.

VANILLA CUPCAKES

2 cups (320 g / 11.3 oz) plain or all-purpose flour

1 ½ cups (330 g / 11.6 oz) sugar

1 tablespoon baking powder

1 teaspoon salt

1 ½ teaspoons powdered gelatin

½ cup (92 g / 3.3 oz) vegetable oil

7 egg yolks (105 g / 3.7 oz)

1 cup (250 mL / 8.5 fl oz) cold water

1 teaspoon vanilla extract

7 egg whites (250 g / 8.9 oz)

½ teaspoon cream of tartar

HEARTS

3 vanilla cupcakes (see above)

Red gel food coloring

1 teaspoon water

MINT BUTTERCREAM FROSTING

1 ½ cups (360 g / 12.7 oz) butter or margarine

7 ½ cups (1 kg / 2.2 pounds) icing sugar or powdered sugar

A few drops peppermint essence (optional)

DECORATION

Heart-shaped sprinkles

VANILLA CUPCAKES

Preheat the oven to 180°C (350°F).

Place the flour, sugar, baking powder, salt, and gelatin in a bowl and stir with a whisk.

Make a well in the center and add the oil, egg yolks, water, and vanilla, but do not mix.

In a separate bowl, whip the egg whites and cream of tartar until they form soft peaks. Beat the flour mixture on low speed until just combined. Fold one third of the egg whites into the flour mixture, then fold in the rest.

Fill three cupcake cups in a cupcake pan and bake for 10-15 minutes. Leave the remaining mixture in the bowl for now. IMPORTANT: Take your three cupcakes and skip ahead to make the hearts before proceeding to the next step.

Fill 18 cups in a cupcake pan with 2 tablespoons each of batter and bake for 4-5 minutes. The mixture should be set on the sides but still runny in the middle. Place your hearts into the centers, pointy side down. Add another tablespoon of vanilla cake mixture over the top of each one, then return to the oven and bake for 5-7 minutes more. Cool completely before frosting.

HEARTS

Crumble the three cooked cupcakes into a bowl. Add red food coloring, one tablespoon of uncooked cake batter, and one teaspoon of water. Mix really well to combine and get an even color.

Take one teaspoon of mixture and roll into a ball. Rest each ball on the palm of your hand; with your other hand, gently press and roll one end of the ball to form a teardrop shape. Using a jumbo pencil sharpener, sharpen the end of a wooden spoon. Press the point gently into the rounded end of the teardrop. This makes the central dip in the hearts. Repeat to make eighteen hearts.

MINT BUTTERCREAM FROSTING

Place the margarine, icing sugar, and peppermint essence in a bowl and mix on low speed until it looks crumbly. Turn speed up to high and whip for one minute. Place the frosting into a piping bag fitted with a star-shaped tip and pipe swirls on top of each cupcake. Scatter some heart-shaped sprinkles onto the frosting. Serve them fresh and wait for the delight as every cupcake reveals a heart.

Video tutorial for this recipe can be found at howtocookthat.net/cookbook

CRAVING
CHOCOLATE

CRAVING CHOCOLATE

Everyone loves chocolate. In fact, worldwide consumption has increased to a mountainous eight million metric tons of chocolate per year! It's no wonder then that some of my biggest crowd-pleasers involve heaps of the stuff. But before we get into all that, there's some important things you need to know... Firstly, not all chocolate is actually chocolate.

REAL VS. FAKE CHOCOLATE

It's important to know the difference between real and fake chocolate in the kitchen. The fail-safe way to know is to simply flip over the packet and read the ingredients. If it contains cocoa butter, you have real chocolate. However, if the ingredient list includes vegetable fat, then it's compound chocolate, or as I call it, fake chocolate.

The main difference between vegetable fat and cocoa butter is the melting point. Cocoa butter melts at just below body temperature, which means it melts in your mouth, allowing the chocolate flavor to hit your taste buds. In comparison, the higher melting point of vegetable fat means that compound chocolate doesn't melt quickly at body temperature, instead leaving a fatty layer on the roof of your mouth, with the result that less flavor reaches your taste buds before you swallow it.

So why would anyone use compound chocolate? Well, it's usually less expensive (which is why those packets of cheap Easter eggs don't taste very nice). It is also easier to work with compound chocolate, allowing bakers to melt and then reset it without the need for any extra steps. And this brings us to tempering.

TEMPERED VS UNTEMPERED

If you were to watch through a microscope as real chocolate was heated up, you'd see all the fat crystals in the cocoa butter melt. Then, as the chocolate cooled and set again, you'd see the fat reforming into one of six different arrangements. The shape of the fat crystal structure affects the melting point and texture of the chocolate.

Think about the cocoa butter in chocolate like a wall built from Lego bricks. The wall can be broken into individual bricks and rebuilt into different patterns of wall design, some of which are stronger than others.

If left to its own devices, melted chocolate sets into an unstable crystal (untempered chocolate), meaning that it remains soft and dull at room temperature. It tastes great, but it melts at 18°C (64°F). You can make it set by putting in the fridge, but as soon as you bring it back to room temperature, it will become soft again, with the result that it will melt in your hands and will not hold its shape.

The good news is that it is possible to encourage stable fat crystals to form so that the chocolate is shiny and crisp at room temperature. This process is called tempering.

HOW DO YOU TEMPER CHOCOLATE?

You can encourage the chocolate crystals to form a stable structure by using one of the following processes. With all methods, it is best to let the chocolate set at room temperature as this allows more of the stable crystal structure to form.

Freeze-dried Cocoa Butter Method

Completely melt your chocolate either in the microwave or a double boiler. If using a microwave, for 300 g (10.6 oz) of chocolate, microwave on high for 30 seconds, then stir, microwave again for 10 seconds, stir, and repeat in 10-second bursts until it is completely melted. Cool until it comes down to the following temperature:

White chocolate: cool to 29-30°C (84-86°F)
Milk chocolate: cool to 31-33°C (88-91°F)
Dark chocolate: cool to 32-35°C (90-95°F)

You can put the bowl of chocolate into a sink full of water to speed up the cooling process, but be careful not to splash any water into the chocolate. Once it is at the right temperature, add in a teaspoon of freeze-dried cocoa butter per 7 ounces (200 g) of chocolate. Stir it through using a spatula. The freeze-dried cocoa butter has the stable crystal structure that we want, and it sets an example for the cocoa butter in the melted chocolate to follow.

Adding the cocoa butter at the right temperature is very important. If you add it when the chocolate is too hot, it will completely melt and you will lose the example pattern. If you add it when it's too cold, the freeze-dried cocoa butter won't mix in and you'll get little white dots in your chocolates.

Block Seeding Method

Set aside a chunk of your tempered chocolate. Melt the rest, then cool to 34°C (94°F). Add in a large piece of tempered chocolate. Stir continuously until the chocolate cools to 32°C (91°F); at that point, remove any of the solid chocolate that hasn't yet melted.

Tabling Method

Completely melt your chocolate. Tip approximately two thirds onto a cool surface such as a marble bench top. Using an offset spatula, spread the chocolate out, then scrape it all back up into a pile, repeating these two steps continuously until the chocolate flows down off the spatula and forms ribbons that stay on top of the pile of chocolate. This step helps to keep the chocolate at an even temperature; as it cools, it will start to thicken.. Scrape the cooled chocolate back into the bowl with the rest of the chocolate and stir through.

Microwave Method

This is not technically tempering, but it keeps the chocolate in temper by not completely melting the fat crystals. Finely grate 300 g (10.6 oz) of milk chocolate and put it into a microwave safe plastic bowl. Do not use a glass or melamine bowl as they get hot in the microwave and will make the temperature too high for this method. Microwave on high for 20 seconds, stir, microwave 10 seconds, stir, microwave 10 seconds, stir, microwave 10 seconds and stir.

Use a candy thermometer as you carefully raise the temperature of the chocolate. (If it gets too hot, the fat crystals will be completely melted.) Use the following temperatures as a guide.

White chocolate: do not go over 29°C (84°F)
Milk chocolate: do not go over 30°C (86°F)
Dark chocolate: do not go over 32°C (90°F)

Tempering Using a Machine

Automatic tempering machines melt the chocolate, allow it to cool to a precise temperature, then reheat it again while slowly stirring it. Taking the chocolate through an exact temperature curve tempers the chocolate. The machine then keeps the chocolate at a constant temperature so it remains liquid and in temper. This allows chocolatiers to work with large amounts of chocolate over several hours without the need to constantly melt and temper chocolate.

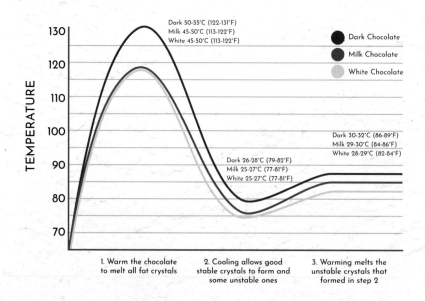

TEMPERATURE

Dark 50-55°C (122-131°F)
Milk 45-50°C (113-122°F)
White 45-50°C (113-122°F)

● Dark Chocolate
● Milk Chocolate
○ White Chocolate

Dark 30-32°C (86-89°F)
Milk 29-30°C (84-86°F)
White 28-29°C (82-84°F)

Dark 26-28°C (79-82°F)
Milk 25-27°C (77-81°F)
White 25-27°C (77-81°F)

1. Warm the chocolate to melt all fat crystals

2. Cooling allows good stable crystals to form and some unstable ones

3. Warming melts the unstable crystals that formed in step 2

WHAT CAN GO WRONG?

Seized Chocolate

Water and chocolate do not get along! If you get any water-based liquid in your chocolate, it will turn into a lumpy, crumbly mess. This is called seized chocolate. Your only hope at this point is to add more liquid, like some cream or milk, and whisk it in to make a ganache instead. You will need to add at least one third of the weight of your chocolate in liquid.

Burnt Chocolate

Chocolate will burn if you heat it above 55°C (130°F). Depending on how burnt it is, chocolate will form a thick crumbly paste and then turn black and start to smoke.

WARM CHOCOLATE MELTING CAKE

Cruising is a terrific way to travel with the family, visit amazing places, and, of course, eat to your heart's content. While on board the Carnival Imagination some years back, I had the privilege of touring the huge ship's kitchen. The pastry chefs, who make literally thousands of these desserts every day, were only too pleased to show me how to make their most popular recipe, the warm chocolate melting cake. Below is a scaled down version perfect for home cooks.

Makes 6 desserts.

CHOCOLATE DECORATION
3.5 oz (100 g) milk chocolate
0.7 oz (20 g) white chocolate

MELTING CAKE
8 oz (230 g) dark chocolate
1 cup (220 g / 7.8 oz) unsalted butter
7 eggs (315 g / 11.1 oz)
6 tablespoons (80 g / 2.8 oz) sugar
½ cup (80 g / 2.8 oz) plain or
    all-purpose flour
1 teaspoon icing sugar or powdered
    sugar for dusting

TO SERVE
Cookie crumbs
Vanilla ice cream
Icing sugar or powdered sugar

CHOCOLATE DECORATION
Temper the milk chocolate (see page 48) and spread it out on some foil. Give the foil a little shake to smooth the top. Melt the white chocolate and put it into a Ziploc bag. Cut off a tiny corner and drizzle it across the milk chocolate. Leave it to set, then break into six large shards.

MELTING CAKE
Preheat the oven to 175°C (350°F). Melt the chocolate and butter in a pan, then set aside to cool.

In a bowl whisk 4 of the eggs with the sugar and the flour until smooth. Add in the remaining 3 eggs and beat to combine. Mix in your chocolate mixture.

Pour into individual ramekins. At this point, you can keep them covered in the fridge for up to 24 hours. Shortly before you're ready to serve, place in a deep baking pan or dish and add water until it is halfway up the sides of the ramekins. Bake for 10-15 minutes or until it is set on the outside but still soft in the middle.

TO SERVE
Add a spoonful of crumbs to one side of a plate. Place a small scoop of vanilla ice cream onto the crumbs and poke a chocolate decoration into the top of the ice cream. Then place a hot dessert alongside, sprinkle with powdered sugar through a sieve, and serve immediately.

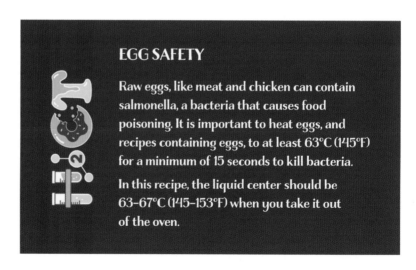

EGG SAFETY

Raw eggs, like meat and chicken can contain salmonella, a bacteria that causes food poisoning. It is important to heat eggs, and recipes containing eggs, to at least 63°C (145°F) for a minimum of 15 seconds to kill bacteria.

In this recipe, the liquid center should be 63–67°C (145–153°F) when you take it out of the oven.

Video tutorial for this recipe can be found at howtocookthat.net/cookbook

CHOCOLATE OBSESSION

Make this incredibly luxurious dessert for a chocolate lover and you'll have a friend for life.

Makes 6.

CHOCOLATE WAVE

10.6 oz (300 g) milk chocolate

Piece of marble or Corian cutting board

STRAWBERRIES

2 tablespoons (30 mL / 1 fl oz) Marsala or brandy

1 ½ cups (200 g / 7 oz) strawberries, finely diced

2 tablespoons (26 g / 0.9 oz) sugar

CHOCOLATE CRUMBLE

3.5 oz (100 g) milk chocolate

¾ cup (80 g / 2.8 oz) hazelnut meal

CHOCOLATE MOUSSE

1 ½ teaspoons powdered gelatin, or 2 gelatin sheets

Bowl of water if using gelatin sheets

½ cup (100 mL / 3.4 fl oz) heavy cream (35 percent fat)

¼ cup (50 g / 1.8 oz) butter or margarine

7 oz (200 g) milk chocolate, melted

Video tutorial for this recipe can be found at howtocookthat.net/cookbook

CHOCOLATE WAVE

Place your marble or Corian board in the freezer for at least 4 hours, preferably overnight.

Melt the milk chocolate, then quickly spread some out in a thin layer on the cold board. Cut three long rectangles of chocolate, each measuring 1½ x 8½ inches (4 x 22 cm). Stack them together, then stand them up on their sides and gently shape into a wave. If it sets too quickly to bend, just take it off the cold surface for a moment to soften and then bend the stack again. Separate them slightly, then immediately place them into the fridge and leave for 2 hours to firm up. Repeat for each dessert.

STRAWBERRIES

Dice the strawberries into small cubes. Place in a pan with the sugar and Marsala. If you prefer, you can leave out the alcohol and use water instead. Simmer for about one minute or until the berry cubes are soft and the sugar is dissolved. Remove from the heat and leave to cool.

CHOCOLATE CRUMBLE

Melt the chocolate in the microwave on high for 1 minute, then stir, microwave 30 seconds, stir, and repeat 30-second bursts stirring each time until melted. Add the hazelnut meal and stir through well. Place in the fridge for 30 minutes. Squash any large clumps to make an even chocolate hazelnut crumble.

CHOCOLATE MOUSSE

Place the gelatin sheets into the bowl of water and leave to soak. If using powdered gelatin, mix with half of the cream and set aside to soften.

Heat the butter and cream in a saucepan until the butter is melted. Squeeze the water out of the gelatin sheets and add them to the pan, or add the softened powdered gelatin, and stir well. Remove from the heat. Pour in the chocolate, leave for a couple of minutes, then whisk together until you have a smooth and even mixture. Cover and cool to room temperature.

Take the cooled chocolate mixture and whip it using electric beaters until it becomes pale and thick. Place into a piping bag and cut about ⅜ inch (1 cm) off the end. Use immediately so that it does not set in the piping bag.

ASSEMBLY

Place one wave of chocolate upright on its side on a plate. At one end, pipe two lines of mousse up the chocolate, leave a 1-inch (2.5 cm) gap, and then pipe two more lines. Add a second chocolate wave, pressing it slightly into the mousse. Make sure you still have a gap between the chocolate where there is no mousse. Repeat and add the third wave.

Add cooled strawberry mixture into the gaps between the chocolate mousse. And finally, spoon chocolate crumble into the ends of the waves. Store in the fridge until ready to serve.

MAGIC CHOCOLATE FLOWER

Bring a theatrical touch to the dining table with this lovely dessert. As you pour the hot crème anglaise into the bowl, the chocolate petals fall open to reveal the delights hidden inside.

CHOCOLATE FLOWER

Per chocolate flower:

3.5 oz (100 g) dark chocolate

Chocolate flower petal template (page 180)

3 sheets of acetate

Silicone hemisphere mold, each cavity ⅓ cup (80 mL / 2.7 fl oz)

1 edible flower

For each inside:

1 small macaron (page 132)

1 raspberry

8 blueberries

1 chocolate truffle

CRÈME ANGLAISE

(Enough for 4 flowers)

¼ cup (50 g / 1.8 oz) sugar

5 egg yolks (90 g / 3.2 oz)

1 vanilla bean or 1 teaspoon vanilla extract

1 cup (250 mL / 8.5 fl oz) heavy cream (35 percent fat)

½ cup (125 mL / 4.2 fl oz) milk

CHOCOLATE FLOWER

Using the chocolate flower template, cut a row of petal-shaped holes out of one sheet of acetate. Place it on top of a second sheet of acetate.

Temper the chocolate (see page 48), then spread a thin layer over the top of the sheet of acetate with the holes. Remove the cut sheet of acetate so that you leave behind just the chocolate petals on the bottom sheet. Working quickly before the chocolate hardens, roll it so that the petals are curved in a half circle. Use cookie cutters or something cylindrical to hold the acetate in place while the chocolate sets. Repeat to make 12 petals for each flower.

Spread out more chocolate on another piece of acetate. When it starts to harden, cut out a 2.5 cm (1 inch) circle for each dessert. Cut each circle in half.

ASSEMBLY

Use a little melted chocolate to secure a macaron to the top of a chocolate truffle. Then, using more chocolate, arrange the fruit on top of the macaron.

Position half the chocolate petals around a silicone hemisphere mold. Use chocolate to add a half circle at the base to hold the petals together. Repeat for the other half of the flower and leave to set.

Take one half of the flower off the silicon hemisphere mold. Put it into a bowl, using some melted chocolate to "glue" it there. Add the assembled chocolate macaron into the center. Carefully add the other half of the flower, using more melted chocolate to fasten it in place.

CRÈME ANGLAISE

Whisk together the sugar and egg yolks in a bowl. Scrape the vanilla bean, then add the seeds and the pod to a saucepan with the cream and milk. Heat until it starts to boil, then remove from the stove and pour about half a cup of hot cream into your egg yolks and whisk well. Pour this egg yolk mixture into the pan of hot cream, whisking as you do so. Refrigerate until ready to serve.

When you're ready to serve, reheat the crème anglaise on low heat to 85°C (185°F). Immediately pour through a sieve into a jug. Take the dessert to the table and pour hot crème anglaise into the bowl. As the chocolate base melts, the flower petals fan open beautifully, creating a dessert experience to delight your senses.

Video tutorial for this recipe can be found at howtocookthat.net/cookbook

SPIRAL CHOCOLATE CARAMEL DOMES

This impressive dessert is perfect for a dinner party as most of the elements can be prepared weeks ahead and stored in the freezer. (Sneaky tip: you can also prepare a double batch of caramel brûlée—freeze half for this dessert and enjoy the rest straight away.)

Makes 12.

LIGHT CHOCOLATE CAKE

1½ tablespoons (20 g / 0.7 oz) sugar
2 egg whites (72 g / 2.5 oz)
⅓ cup (80 g / 2.8 oz) sugar
5 medium egg yolks (75 g / 2.6 oz)
¼ cup (30 g / 1.1 oz) cocoa powder
¼ cup (40 g / 1.4 oz) plain or
   all-purpose flour
2 tablespoons (30 g / 1.1 oz)
   margarine or butter, melted

VANILLA SYRUP

⅓ cup (75 g / 2.6 oz) sugar
½ cup (110 mL / 3.7 fl oz) water
½ teaspoon vanilla extract

CARAMEL CRÈME BRÛLÉE

1½ teaspoons powdered gelatin or
   2 gelatin sheets
Water to soften gelatin
1 tablespoon (15 mL / 0.5 fl oz) water
3 tablespoons (40 g / 1.4 oz) sugar
⅓ cup (100 mL / 3.4 fl oz) milk
⅓ cup (100 mL / 3.4 fl oz) heavy
   cream (35 percent fat)
6 egg yolks (90 g / 3.2 oz)
2 tablespoons (25 g / 0.9 oz) sugar

SALTED BUTTER CARAMEL

1 cup (200 g / 7 oz) sugar
¼ cup (37 mL / 1.3 fl oz) water
½ cup (100 g / 3.5 oz) heavy cream
   (35 percent fat)
½ cup (120 g / 4.2 oz) butter
A pinch of sea salt

CHOCOLATE MOUSSE

1 whole egg (50 g / 1.76 oz)
1½ egg yolks (22 g / 0.8 oz)
1 tablespoon (45 g / 1.6 oz) sugar
½ tablespoon (7.5 g / 0.3 oz) water

LIGHT CHOCOLATE CAKE

Preheat the oven to 180°C (350°F).

Whip the egg whites with 1½ tablespoons of sugar until soft peaks form. Add the remaining sugar to the yolks and whip until pale and fluffy. Fold one third of the whites into the yolks. Sift the flour and cocoa powder over the top and fold together. Add the rest of the egg whites and fold gently to combine.

Mix a quarter of this mixture in with the melted butter. Add the rest of the egg mixture and fold together. Do not overmix.

Pour into a lined 10 x 15 inch (25 x 38 cm) cake pan (baking tray), spread batter, and bake for around 10 minutes or until a knife inserted into the center comes out clean.

VANILLA SYRUP

Combine all the ingredients and heat in a pan until the sugar is dissolved. Once your chocolate cake is cooked, leave it in the cake pan and pour the syrup over the top.

CARAMEL CRÈME BRÛLÉE

Place the gelatin sheets in a bowl of water and set aside. If using powdered gelatin, quickly mix with 1 tablespoon of water and leave to soften.

Put 1 tablespoon of water and 3 tablespoons of sugar in a pan, then stir to make sure all the sugar is wet. Heat over high heat until the bubbles start to slow and the mixture turns into a golden caramel. Add the milk and cream, being careful of the steam. Stir until the caramel is dissolved.

In a separate bowl, whip together the egg yolks and remaining 2 tablespoons of sugar. Whisk in half a cup of the hot cream. Add the yolk mixture into the pan with the rest of the hot cream, whisking as you do so. Heat for just one minute more; note that if you overheat this mixture it will curdle. Remove from the heat, then add the gelatin and stir until it melts.

Line a 7.5 x 10 inch (19 x 25 cm) baking pan or container with foil. Pour in the brûlée mixture and freeze overnight.

SALTED BUTTER CARAMEL

Place the sugar and water into a pan and stir, making sure all the sugar is wet. Heat over high heat until the bubbles start to slow and the mixture turns into a golden caramel. Add the cream, butter, and salt.

⅔ cup (150 mL / 5.1 fl oz) heavy cream (35 percent fat)

3.7 oz (105 g) dark chocolate, melted

Silicone hemisphere mold, each cavity ⅓ cup (80 mL / 2.7 fl oz)

CHOCOLATE MIRROR GLAZE

Makes more than you need, store the excess in a Ziploc bag in the freezer.

½ tablespoon (10 g / 0.4 oz) powdered gelatin

3 tablespoons (45 g / 1.6 oz) cold water

⅔ cup (150 g / 5.3 oz) sugar

3 tablespoons (45 g / 1.6 oz) additional water

⅓ cup (100 g / 3.5 oz) heavy cream (35 percent fat)

⅓ cup (50 g / 1.7 oz) cocoa powder

⅓ cup (125 g / 4.4 oz) glucose syrup or light corn syrup

CHOCOLATE SPIRAL

3.5 oz (100 g) white compound chocolate

Cake turntable or lazy Susan

Piping bag

Stir over high heat until a teaspoon of mixture dropped into a glass of cold water is sufficiently thick to form a very soft blob.

Pour into a heatproof container and leave to cool.

CHOCOLATE MOUSSE

Make the mousse after all of the above elements are ready.

Using an electric mixer, beat the egg and extra yolks on high speed until they become fluffy and pale. Place the sugar and water into a pan and heat to 118°C (244°F) on a candy thermometer. With the mixer running, pour the hot sugar into the eggs. Continue to beat until the sides of the bowl feel cool.

Whip the cream to soft peaks; fold in the melted chocolate and then the egg mixture.

CHOCOLATE MIRROR GLAZE

Mix together the gelatin and water and set aside. Put the sugar, additional water, and cream into a pan and heat until the sugar is dissolved. Sift in the cocoa powder and whisk together. Add the gelatin and stir until it has melted. Add the glucose syrup and mix well. Allow the glaze to cool before using.

CHOCOLATE SPIRAL

Melt the chocolate in the microwave on high for 60 seconds. Stir and repeat with additional 30-second bursts, stirring each time until it is completely melted. Place the chocolate into a piping bag or Ziploc bag and cut off a tiny corner from the end.

Put a circle of baking paper onto a cake turntable or lazy Susan and spin it. Put the tip of the piping bag in the center, squeeze gently while moving the bag toward the edge of the spinning circle to create a spiral. Move the baking paper onto the counter to set and repeat for the remaining desserts.

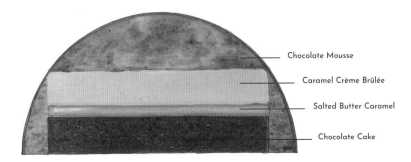

Chocolate Mousse

Caramel Crème Brûlée

Salted Butter Caramel

Chocolate Cake

ASSEMBLY

Cut twelve 5 cm (2 inch) circles out of the cake and the frozen brûlée. Top each circle of cake with a spoonful of caramel and then add a frozen brûlée.

Place a tablespoon of chocolate mousse into the base of the hemisphere mold. If you do not have a silicone hemisphere mold, you can use small bowls with a similar volume, i.e., ⅓ cup per bowl. Add a stack into the center of each dessert, brûlée side down. Push down into the mousse until the cake is flush with the top of the mold. Add more mousse to fill any gaps and level off. Freeze for at least 3 hours.

Bring your glaze to the right temperature by microwaving in 10-second bursts if required. It should be warm enough to be a liquid, but not hot or it will melt the outside of the dessert and slide off. Take the desserts out of the freezer and remove from the mold. If you used bowls instead of a silicon mold, you'll need to heat the outside of the bowl in a container of warm water, remove the dessert from the bowl, and then return it to the freezer for 30 minutes.

In a baking pan, put the frozen dessert on top of a small cookie cutter to elevate it, then ladle glaze over the top. The cold dessert will set a thin layer of the glaze while the excess runs off. Carefully lift the glazed dessert onto a plate and top with a chocolate spiral. Refrigerate until defrosted and serve to your delighted guests.

Video tutorial for this recipe can be found at howtocookthat.net/cookbook

MELTING CHOCOLATE 'N' PEANUT BALL

This dessert is rich, gooey, crunchy, and impressive. Pour on the hot caramel sauce and watch as the top of the ball melts open! Then let your spoon dive into the rich goodies hidden inside.

Makes 4 spheres.

SPHERES

14.1 oz (400 g) dark chocolate

Silicone hemisphere mold with six cavities, each holding ⅓ cup (80 mL / 2.7 fl oz)

CRÉMEUX

4.8 oz (135 g) dark chocolate

3.9 oz (110 g) milk chocolate

4 egg yolks (60 g / 2.1 oz)

2 tablespoons (30 g / 1.1 oz) sugar

1 cup (225 mL / 7.6 fl oz) heavy cream (35 percent fat)

PEANUT BRITTLE

1 cup (216 g / 7.6 oz) caster sugar or superfine sugar

¼ cup (65 mL / 2.1 fl oz) water

⅔ cup (100 g / 3.5 oz) unsalted roasted peanuts

POWDERED PEANUT BUTTER

2 tablespoons (30 g / 1.1 oz) smooth peanut butter

3 tablespoons (28 g / 1 oz) maltodextrin powder

EASY CARAMEL SAUCE

⅓ cup (100 mL / 3.4 fl oz) heavy cream (35 percent fat)

⅓ cup (75 g / 2.6 oz) butter

½ cup (100 g / 3.5 oz) brown sugar

ASSEMBLY

Edible flowers (optional)

SPHERES

This dessert requires real chocolate, so make sure the ingredients include cocoa butter and then follow the tempering instructions on page 48. Pour your tempered chocolate into six hemisphere molds and spread it out so that it covers the edges. Put some foil onto the counter and turn the mold upside down, shaking it to let the excess chocolate drip out onto the foil. Flip the mold back over and use a spatula to wipe the top clean. Turn it over once again and place upside down on baking paper to set.

CRÉMEUX

Put the dark and milk chocolate into a bowl and place a sieve over the top. In a separate bowl, whisk together the egg yolks and sugar. Heat the cream in a pan until it just starts to boil. Remove from the heat and whisk ¼ cup of hot cream to the egg yolks to temper them. Tip the egg yolk mixture into the pan with the rest of the cream and whisk together. Stir over high heat for about one minute or until it reaches 85°C (185°F). Do not overheat or it will split and become lumpy. Immediately remove from the heat and pour the mixture through the sieve onto the chocolate. Wait for two minutes, then whisk the now-melted chocolate into the cream. Cool to room temperature.

PEANUT BRITTLE

Preheat the oven to 100°C (200°F / Low). Spread the peanuts out onto a baking sheet lined with baking paper and place in the oven to warm.

Place the sugar and water in a saucepan over high heat, stirring until the sugar dissolves. Using a wet pastry brush, wash down the sides of the pan to remove any sugar crystals. Continue to heat unstirred until the bubbles slow and it starts to turn golden. Remove from the heat and check if it is ready by dropping a small spoonful into a glass of cold water. If it's hot enough, it will set hard instantly. If not, simply return to the heat and repeat the test in 30 seconds.

Take the peanuts out of the oven and pour the liquid hot sugar over the top. Using a fork, quickly move the peanuts around, making sure they are all covered. Then leave to cool.

Break into small chunks and store in an airtight container until needed.

POWDERED PEANUT BUTTER

Stir the maltodextrin powder into the peanut butter one tablespoon at a time until it resembles wet sand.

EASY CARAMEL SAUCE

Put the cream, butter, and brown sugar into a bowl and stir. Microwave on high for 2 minutes, stir, then microwave 1 more minute and stir again. Repeat these 1-minute bursts, stirring each time until the sauce is hot and thickened. Pour into a heatproof jug and use while hot.

ASSEMBLY

Preheat the oven to 180°C (350°F). Place a baking sheet into the oven to warm up.

Remove the chocolate hemispheres from the silicone mold by stretching the mold slightly to loosen the edges, then gently pushing on the back in the center.

Place a spoonful of powdered peanut butter into the middle of each plate. Add a chocolate hemisphere on top. Nearly fill the hemisphere with chocolate crémeux and pile on some peanut brittle. Add an edible flower on top.

Take another hemisphere and quickly touch the rim to the hot baking sheet to melt a tiny amount of chocolate. Then place this on top of the first hemisphere to make a ball. Serve to the table and pour hot caramel sauce over the ball allowing it to drip down the sides. The sauce will melt the chocolate and cause the ball to open up, creating a wonderful experience for guests.

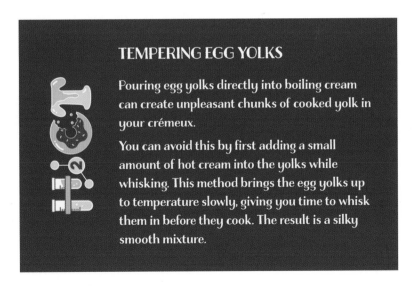

TEMPERING EGG YOLKS

Pouring egg yolks directly into boiling cream can create unpleasant chunks of cooked yolk in your crémeux.

You can avoid this by first adding a small amount of hot cream into the yolks while whisking. This method brings the egg yolks up to temperature slowly, giving you time to whisk them in before they cook. The result is a silky smooth mixture.

Video tutorial for this recipe can be found at howtocookthat.net/cookbook

Melting Chocolate 'n' Peanut Ball

HAZELNUT CHOCOLATE DESSERT SLICE

Every now and then you find a dessert that is just perfect. It looks amazing, tastes divine, has a variety of textures, and, of course, the ingredient list includes chocolate. The only downside of this beautiful dessert is that it's not particularly quick or easy to make. However, don't let that discourage you as it can be made well ahead of your planned event and frozen, thereby reducing unnecessary stress on the day.

Makes 20 large servings.

CHOCOLATE CHANTILLY CREAM

2 cups (500 g / 17.6 oz) heavy cream (35 percent fat)

6.4 oz (180 g) milk chocolate, chopped

CRISPY BASE

4.9 oz (140 g) milk chocolate

2.5 oz (70 g) dark chocolate

½ cup (180 g / 6.4 oz) Nutella

1 cup (30 g / 1.1 oz) Rice Krispies (Rice Bubbles or other crispy puffed rice cereal)

HAZELNUT DACQUOISE

1 ½ cups (200 g / 7.1 oz) icing sugar or powdered sugar

2 cups (200 g / 7.1 oz) hazelnut meal

7 egg whites (250 g / 8.8 oz)

¼ cup (60 g / 2.1 oz) sugar

A pinch of cream of tartar

¾ cup (100 g / 3.5 oz) hazelnuts, roughly chopped

CHOCOLATE CRÉMEUX

7.1 oz (200 g) milk chocolate

9.5 oz (270 g) dark chocolate

8 egg yolks (120 g / 4.2 oz)

¼ cup (60 g / 2.1 oz) sugar

2 ¼ cup (550 g / 19.4 oz) heavy cream (35 percent fat)

CHOCOLATE RECTANGLES

14.1 oz (400 g) milk chocolate

ASSEMBLY

20 roasted hazelnuts (18 g / 0.6 oz)

3.5 oz (100 g) milk chocolate

Pastry comb

CHOCOLATE CHANTILLY CREAM

Bring your cream to a boil and pour it over the chopped milk chocolate. Leave it to sit for a couple of minutes, then whisk until smooth. Place in the fridge overnight. Whisk with an electric mixer until it becomes a little lighter in color and forms smooth peaks.

CRISPY BASE

Melt the chocolates in the microwave on high for one minute, then stir, microwave 30 seconds, stir again, and repeat in 30-second bursts until melted. Stir in the Nutella. Add the Rice Krispies and stir well.

Pour onto a baking sheet lined with baking paper. Place baking paper over the top; then, using a rolling pin, flatten the mixture out to make a rectangle 12 x 16 inches (30 x 40 cm) in size. Place it in the freezer.

HAZELNUT DACQUOISE

Preheat the oven to 170°C (340°F).

Sift the icing sugar and hazelnut meal together through a course sieve. In a separate bowl, whisk together the egg whites, sugar, and cream of tartar until stiff peaks form. Gently fold the icing sugar and hazelnut meal into the egg whites.

Spread the mixture into a lined pan 12 x 16 inches (30 x 40 cm) and sprinkle with chopped hazelnuts. Bake for around 20 minutes or until golden. Sprinkle with a little icing sugar and leave to cool.

CHOCOLATE CRÉMEUX

Break up the chocolate and place in a bowl with a sieve resting over the top. In a separate bowl, whisk together the yolks and the sugar. Put the cream in a saucepan and bring to a boil.

Whisk a quarter of a cup of hot cream into the egg yolks, then tip the yolk mixture into the pan with the rest of the cream and mix well.

Return to the heat and stir constantly until it reaches 85°C (185°F). Immediately remove from the stove and pour through the sieve over the chocolate.

Leave it for a couple of minutes to melt, then whisk to combine.

CHOCOLATE RECTANGLES

Take a 45 inch (115 cm) sheet of aluminum foil and mark 2.2 inch (5.5 cm) increments along the top edge and 3.75 inches (9.5 cm) down the side. Temper the chocolate (see page 48), then spread it out thinly on the aluminum foil to make a large rectangle. Once it is firm but not yet hard, cut the chocolate with a knife. Use a ruler and the guidelines that you drew to make 40 perfectly even rectangles. Place in the fridge until crisp.

ASSEMBLY

Line a 30 x 40 cm (12 x 16 inch) container with plastic wrap along the bottom and sides. (You can use two smaller containers if necessary.) Reserve 1 cup of crémeux, then pour the rest into the container and jiggle to smooth. Trim the dacquoise to fit snuggly into the container and place on top of the crémeux, hazelnut side down. Spread on the remaining 1 cup of crémeux; finally, top with the crispy base. Freeze for at least 3 hours.

Temper the milk chocolate and pour it on one side of a strip of acetate, using a pastry comb to spread it out into thin, even lines. Curve the acetate slightly by placing the ends into cups and leave it to set.

Take the base out of the freezer, flip it over, and remove it from the container. Leave a 1 cm (0.4 inch) gap at each edge and cover the top with 20 chocolate rectangles neatly lined up with each other.

Put a long sharp knife in a tall container of hot water. Use the hot knife to cut rectangles the same size as your chocolate.

Place the Chantilly cream in a piping bag fitted with a round nozzle and pipe six dots on top of each rectangle. Top with another rectangle of chocolate. Pipe a swirl of Chantilly cream in the center on top, then add half a roasted hazelnut and a chocolate swirl.

Hazelnut Chocolate Dessert Slice

CHOCOLATE PISTACHIO DOME

The galley on a cruise ship is unimaginably huge. The area for the pastry chefs alone is bigger than most restaurant kitchens. On my second visit to a ship's galley, I was lucky enough to spend a whole day filming with the ship's talented chefs as they made thousands of these desserts. With their permission, I have adapted their original recipe to suit home cooks.

Makes 12 domes.

CHOCOLATE DECORATIONS
Acetate

3.5 oz (100 g) dark chocolate

1 tablespoon (10 g / 0.4 oz) cocoa butter

Green oil-based food coloring

3.5 oz (100 g) white chocolate

ALMOND AND PISTACHIO NOUGATINE
⅓ cup (90 g / 3.3 oz) butter

3 tablespoons (63 g / 2.2 oz) glucose syrup or light corn syrup

¾ cup (120 g / 4.2 oz) icing sugar or powdered sugar

½ teaspoon cinnamon

¼ teaspoon pectin (you can leave this out, but it alters the texture)

⅔ cup (66 g / 2.3 oz) flaked almonds

⅔ cup (66 g / 2.3 oz) pistachios, chopped

PISTACHIO PASTE
⅓ cup (70 g / 2.5 oz) sugar

⅓ cup (60 g / 2.1 oz) blanched almonds

2 tablespoons (20 g / 0.7 oz) pistachios

¼ cup (45 g / 1.6 oz) sunflower seed oil

Tiny pinch of salt

PISTACHIO CREAM
1 teaspoon powdered gelatin

1 tablespoon (15 mL / 0.5 fl oz) heavy cream (35 percent fat)

1 tablespoon (15 mL / 0.5 fl oz) milk

1 tablespoon (15 mL / 0.5 fl oz) heavy cream (35 percent fat)

2 teaspoons (8 g / 0.3 oz) sugar

1 egg yolk (15 g / 0.5 oz)

CHOCOLATE DECORATIONS

Temper the dark chocolate (see page 48), then spread it out thinly onto a 12 x 30 cm (5 x 12 inch) strip of acetate. Lift the acetate and move it to a clean area on the bench so you have a long rectangle of chocolate. Using a knife, cut across to make triangles. Curve and place inside a cylinder to set.

Melt the cocoa butter and stir in a drop of green food coloring. Paint the green cocoa butter onto your acetate in long brush strokes, creating subtle stripes. Using a fork with the middle two prongs bent upwards, make swirls in the green cocoa butter.

Temper the white chocolate, then pour it over the cocoa butter, using a palette knife to spread it out evenly. When the chocolate is starting to set but is not yet firm, cut it into 1.5 x 5 cm (½ x 2 inch) rectangles.

ALMOND AND PISTACHIO NOUGATINE

Preheat the oven to 180°C (350°F).

Heat the butter and glucose syrup in a pan. Once the butter is melted, mix in the icing sugar, cinnamon, and pectin. Stir in the almonds and pistachios. Place small scoopfuls into a silicone muffin tin and bake for 10–15 minutes or until golden brown. Allow to cool, then pop them out of the muffin tin and store in an airtight container until needed.

PISTACHIO PASTE

Place all the ingredients in a blender and process until smooth. Makes 5 tablespoons, which is more than is necessary, but you'll struggle to get smaller quantities to blend into a smooth paste.

PISTACHIO CREAM

Mix the powdered gelatin with 1 tablespoon of cream and set aside.

Put the milk plus the second amount of cream and sugar into a pan and heat until it is just starting to boil. Whisk a small amount of hot cream into the egg yolks. Pour this mixture into the pan with the rest of the cream and heat until it reaches 84°C (183°F). Add the pistachio paste and stir until smooth. Remove from the heat, then stir in the gelatin and mix until it is melted. Add the white chocolate and butter and continue to stir until smooth. Add a few drops of green food coloring to resemble the color of pistachios.

Pour into mini hemisphere molds or domed ice cube trays and place in the freezer overnight.

1 ½ tablespoons of pistachio paste (see the previous page)

1.8 oz (50 g) white chocolate

2 teaspoons (8 g / 0.3 oz) butter

Green gel food coloring

Mini ½ tablespoon-size (7.5 mL / 0.25 fl oz) hemisphere molds

ALMOND CAKE

4 tablespoons (32 g / 1.1 oz) icing sugar or powdered sugar

4 tablespoons (52 g / 1.8 oz) butter

4 eggs (200 g / 7 oz)

4 tablespoons (25 g / 0.9 oz) ground almonds

½ cup (80 g / 2.8 oz) plain or all-purpose flour

1 teaspoon baking powder

CHOCOLATE MOUSSE

3 tablespoons (40 g / 1.4 oz) sugar

4 egg yolks (60 g / 2.1 oz)

¼ cup (60 mL / 2 fl oz) milk

¼ cup (60 mL / 2.1 fl oz) heavy cream (35 percent fat)

4.6 oz (130 g) of 70 percent dark chocolate

Additional 1 ½ cups (360 mL / 12.2 fl oz) heavy cream (35 percent fat), whipped

Silicone hemisphere mold, each cavity 80 mL (2.7 fl oz)

CHOCOLATE GLAZE

See page 59

ASSEMBLY

½ cup (120 mL / 4 fl oz) heavy cream (35 percent fat), whipped

½ cup (80 g / 2.8 oz) pistachios, roughly chopped

12 whole pistachios, shelled

Gold luster dust

Chocolate sauce

ALMOND CAKE

Using an electric mixer, beat together the icing sugar and butter until smooth. Add the eggs and almonds and mix again, then add the flour and baking powder and stir until just combined. Pour into a lined 18 x 25 cm (7 x 10 inch) baking pan, spread batter out, and bake for 10 minutes or until a knife inserted into the center comes out clean.

CHOCOLATE MOUSSE

Whisk together the sugar and the egg yolks. Heat the milk and cream in a saucepan until it just comes to a boil. Take a small amount of hot cream and whisk it into the egg yolks. Tip the yolks back into the pan with the rest of the hot cream and stir while heating to 84°C (183°F). Immediately remove from the heat and add in your chocolate. Leave for a few minutes until the chocolate melts, then whisk until combined. Add a third of the whipped cream and mix it through. Allow the mixture to cool to 44°C (110°F), then fold in the rest of the whipped cream.

Pour into hemisphere molds, not quite to the top. Allow it to start to set, then add a frozen pistachio cream into the center of each one, followed by an almond nougatine biscuit and a circle of almond cake. Place in the freezer overnight.

CHOCOLATE GLAZE

See page 59.

ASSEMBLY

Unmold the desserts and glaze following the instructions on page 60. Carefully lift each dessert, touching only the underside of the base, and use your other hand to add chopped pistachios around the lower edge. Put onto a plate, add a dollop of whipped cream plus your chocolate decorations and a couple of pistachios dusted with gold luster dust on top. Pipe two lines and few dots of chocolate sauce to decorate the plate. Defrost in the fridge before serving.

Video tutorial for this recipe can be found at howtocookthat.net/cookbook

Chocolate Pistachio Dome

DECADENT CHOCOLATE MOUSSE CAKE

This decadent chocolate cake has a crunchy cookie crumble, velvety smooth chocolate mousse, fluffy Italian meringue, and gooey salted caramel. All these different textures morph into mouthfuls of "mmms" and "ahhs." It's a guaranteed crowd-pleaser every time!
You can start making this dessert well ahead, leaving time on the day of your gathering to relax and enjoy yourself. I'd suggest making the crunchy cookie crumb, chocolate cake, and salted caramel on day one. Prepare the mousse and assemble on day two, leaving only the Italian meringue, decorating, and of course eating on day three.

8-10 slices.

CRUNCHY COOKIE CRUMBLE

1 teaspoon cornstarch or corn flour

1 teaspoon salt

⅔ cup (105 g / 3.7 oz) plain or all-purpose flour

½ cup (105 g / 3.7 oz) sugar

⅔ cup (80 g / 2.8 oz) cocoa powder

6 tablespoons (80 g / 2.8 oz) melted butter

12.4 oz (350 g) milk chocolate to coat

RICH CHOCOLATE CAKE

1.5 times the recipe on page 32:

10.6 oz (300 g) dark chocolate with 70 percent cocoa

2 cups (470 g / 17 oz) margarine or butter

12 large eggs (540 g / 19 oz)

3 ½ cups (730 g / 25.8 oz) caster sugar or superfine sugar

2 cups (300 g / 10.6 oz) plain or all-purpose flour

6 tablespoons (45 g / 1.6 oz) cocoa powder

2 ½ teaspoons baking powder

SALTED CARAMEL

(Makes 2 cups. It's difficult to measure the temperature accurately with less.)

1 ½ cups (325 g / 11.5 oz) sugar

¼ cup (60 mL / 2 fl oz) water

1 cup (350 g / 12.4 oz) glucose syrup or light corn syrup

CRUNCHY COOKIE CRUMBLE

Preheat the oven to 180°C (350°F).

Put the cornstarch, salt, flour, sugar, and cocoa powder into a bowl and stir until combined. Add the melted butter and continue to mix it until it's a crumbly dough.

Sprinkle chunks of cookie dough onto a baking sheet lined with baking paper and bake for 20 minutes. They will be quite soft when you first remove them from the oven but will crisp up as they cool. Once cold, tip half into an airtight container for later.

Break the milk chocolate into pieces and place in a bowl. Microwave on high for 1 minute, stir, then microwave 30 seconds, stir again, and repeat in 30-second bursts until it is completely melted. Pour half the crumbs into the bowl of melted chocolate and mix until they are coated. Spread out on a lined baking sheet and place in the refrigerator.

RICH CHOCOLATE CAKE

Make one and a half times my Rich Chocolate Cake recipe (see page 32) and bake it in two 10 x 15 inch (25.5 x 38 cm) lined cake pans for 15-20 minutes.

SALTED CARAMEL

Combine the water, sugar, and glucose syrup in a pan. Place over high heat and stir until the sugar is dissolved. Using a wet pastry brush, wash any sugar off the sides of the pan. Leave it to boil unstirred for 4-6 minutes or until it has a golden caramel color. Add the milk and cream, being careful of the burst of steam. At first the caramel will set because the liquid is cool, but continue stirring until the caramel melts completely.

Let the mixture boil unstirred until it reaches 107°C (224°F) on a candy thermometer—this will take about 2-3 minutes. Strain through a sieve into a heatproof bowl. Add in the salt, then stir through and leave the mixture to cool.

CHOCOLATE MOUSSE

Put the sheets of gelatin into the bowl of cool water to soak. If using powdered gelatin, quickly mix with 3 tablespoons (45 mL/1.5 fl oz) of the milk and set aside.

1 cup (250 mL / 8.5 fl oz) heavy cream
   (35 percent fat)
½ cup (125 mL / 4.2 fl oz) milk
Salt to taste
Candy thermometer

CHOCOLATE MOUSSE

(Makes 12 cups)

6 sheets gelatin or 1½ tablespoons
   powdered gelatin
Bowl of water if using gelatin sheets
1 ½ cups (375 mL / 12.7 fl oz) milk
3 tablespoons (60 g / 2.1 oz) glucose
   syrup or light corn syrup
6 large egg yolks (94 g / 3.3 oz)
22 oz (625 g) milk or dark chocolate
3 ½ cups (845 g / 29.8 oz) heavy
   cream (35 percent fat), whipped

ITALIAN MERINGUE

Half the recipe on page 36:

1 ½ egg whites (45 g / 1.6 oz)
⅛ teaspoon cream of tartar
2 tablespoons water (32.5 mL /
   1.1 fl oz)
Candy thermometer

ASSEMBLY

½ cup (125 mL / 4.23 fl oz) milk
4 chocolate bars
¾ cup (100 g / 3.5 oz) strawberries,
   washed
Edible flowers
8-inch (20 cm) cake ring
10-inch (25.5 cm) cake board
28 x 10 inch (70 x 25 cm) sheet of
   acetate

Place the milk and glucose syrup in a large bowl and microwave on high until it bubbles. In a separate bowl, whisk the egg yolks with a little of the hot milk mixture to temper them. Add the rest of the hot milk mixture, whisking as you do so. Microwave for 5 seconds more. Squeeze the gelatin sheets to get rid of as much water as you can, then add them (or the softened powdered gelatin) into the milk mixture and stir until melted.

Pour this mixture over the chocolate and leave it for a couple of minutes until it melts. Stir well with a whisk until your mixture is smooth. Leave to cool to room temperature.

Fold in the whipped cream and use immediately or the mousse will set.

ITALIAN MERINGUE

Shortly before assembly, make a half batch of Italian meringue (directions on page 36).

ASSEMBLY

Level the cakes and cut two 8 inch (20 cm) circles from each cake. Reserve the cake offcuts as you will need them later.

Place a 20 cm (8 inch) cake ring onto a cake board and line with acetate. Beware: your mousse will seep out the bottom if your cake ring isn't totally flat on the board. To keep this from happening, put about ¼ cup of mousse in the bottom, ensuring it is around all the edges, and place in the freezer for a few minutes so that it firms up quickly and seals any little gaps.

Place a layer of cake into the bottom of the cake ring, then sprinkle 2 tablespoons of milk over the cake layer. Add a handful of chocolate-coated cookie chunks. Drizzle on some divine salted caramel. Cover with 2½ cups or 625 mL (21 fl oz) of chocolate mousse.

Continue to layer it up in this manner all the way to the top. Refrigerate for at least 3 hours, preferably overnight.

Chop the chocolate bars into triangular chunks. If they contain caramel, you may need to put them in the freezer to make them easier to handle.

Remove the cake ring and peel off the acetate from the outside of the cake. Add caramel around the top edge, allowing some to drip down the sides of the cake.

On top of the cake, pile some cake offcuts across the center, then add crunchy cookie crumble on both sides.

Generously spoon Italian meringue across the middle so that it covers the cake offcuts. Toast the meringue using a blowtorch, then top with strawberries, edible flowers, and the chopped chocolate bars.

Video tutorial for this recipe can be found at howtocookthat.net/cookbook

Decadent Chocolate Mousse Cake

CHOCOLATE CRÉMEUX WITH RASPBERRIES

Chocolate crémeux, a rich creamy chocolate custard, is a versatile element which can be used in a variety of desserts. It is not as sweet as ganache but is richer than a mousse. In the words of one of my friends: "This is the best thing I have ever tasted."

Makes 9 glasses (250 mL / 8.4 fl oz) each.

CHOCOLATE CRÉMEUX
7.1 oz (200 g) milk chocolate
9.5 oz (270 g) dark chocolate
8 egg yolks (120 g / 4.2 oz)
¼ cup (60 g / 2.12 oz) sugar
2 ¼ cups (550 g / 19.4 oz) heavy cream (35 percent fat)

RASPBERRY JELLY (JELL-O)
Three (85 g / 3 oz) boxes of raspberry jelly crystals (Jell-O)
2 ½ cups (250 g / 8.8 oz) fresh or frozen raspberries

CHOCOLATE DECORATION
3.5 oz (100 g) milk chocolate
Acetate

CHOCOLATE CRÉMEUX

Break up the chocolate and place in a bowl with a sieve resting over the top. In a separate bowl, whisk together the egg yolks and sugar. Pour the cream into a pan and heat until it just comes to a boil.

Whisk ¼ cup of hot cream into the egg yolks. Add this egg yolk mixture back into the pan of hot cream and whisk immediately.

Return to the heat, stirring constantly until just before it reaches 85°C (185°F). Remove from the heat and immediately pour through your sieve over the chocolate. Be careful not to overheat your crémeux as it will split—meaning the oil and water in the cream will separate. So instead of a smooth, creamy, rich chocolate custard, if that happens, you will have an oily mess.

Push your chocolate down so it is all covered and leave for a couple of minutes to melt. Whisk together to combine.

Place small drinking glasses in a muffin tin on an angle and fill halfway with crémeux. Refrigerate until set.

RASPBERRY JELLY (JELL-O)

Make the raspberry jelly (Jell-O) according to the directions on the packet. Allow it to cool to room temperature. Remove your glasses of set crémeux from the muffin tin. Choose the best nine raspberries and set aside for on top of the dessert. Divide the rest of the raspberries between the glasses and add raspberry jelly (Jell-O) up to the same level as the top of the crémeux.

CHOCOLATE DECORATION

Roll a sheet of acetate into a cylinder and place a drinking glass or cookie cutter on either end to hold it in place. Draw a line on the acetate where it overlaps, then unroll it and lay it flat on the bench.

Temper your chocolate (see page 48) and spread it out evenly in a rectangle, but don't cover the area of acetate that overlaps. Use a knife or toothed icing comb to create thin strips of chocolate. Roll the acetate up again so that these chocolate strips form a circle. Leave in the refrigerator to set, using the two glasses to hold it in place.

ASSEMBLY

Once the jelly (Jell-O) is set, add a circle of chocolate to each dessert using a raspberry to hold it in place.

Video tutorial for this recipe can be found at howtocookthat.net/cookbook

ART ON
A PLATE

ART ON A PLATE

Eating is an experience that uses all of our senses. Taste is the obvious one, with five different taste receptors: sweet, salty, sour, bitter, and umami. However, our sense of smell also greatly enhances our ability to enjoy different flavors. The human nose has around four hundred types of scent receptors, allowing us to distinguish between a trillion different odors!

We also cannot overlook the importance of sight (pun intended). Scientists have studied the effect of plating the same dish in two different ways. It will probably come as no surprise that consumers were willing to pay more for the meal that was artistically plated. But what is really interesting is that the beautifully plated dish was consistently rated as better tasting, even though it was the same food.

What about our hearing, then? Have you ever stopped to consider how sound affects your eating habits? Studies have shown that turning up the volume of music from a reasonable level of 72dB to 88dB actually causes people to drink and eat faster. Likewise, lab rats were found to consume more when subjected to a noisy environment. Some restaurants play faster music to encourage people to eat faster and more rapidly vacate their seats, while others play music with a slow tempo so patrons eat slower, consequently staying longer and spending more money on food and drinks. And to top it off, playing stereotypical French or German music resulted in greater sales of French or German wines, respectively.

Finally, our sense of touch is important in any dining experience. This is because we feel the texture of food in our mouths. Would you prefer a rubbery crème brûlée or one that is soft and melts in your mouth? Our hands do also play a part, though, and not just with finger food—one study found people consistently rated food as tasting better when it was served with heavier cutlery.

Desserts are like a playground when it comes to our senses. You can have lots of fun by completely changing the shape, color, and form of your food. This can totally transform the eating experience. Take the dessert tubes in this chapter, for example... Your guests are guaranteed to giggle at the slurping sounds they make when eating. We've seen people return time and again for "just one more" dessert tube. The pure enjoyment of the experience makes them so much more fun than the very same dessert just served in a bowl.

Interactive and artistic desserts are memorable and create a relaxed atmosphere where conversation and laughter flows. If you want it to last longer, don't forget to play some slow-paced music. And if you find yourself without quite enough for everyone, you can always try turning the volume down.

CHOCOLATE CHEESE BOARD

Are you a cheese lover? Then you probably know the feeling of excitement when a host brings out a board covered in amazing cheeses and crackers for dessert. However, if you have a sweet tooth like mine, then even the loveliest cheeseboard just doesn't quite hit the spot. To solve this conundrum, I've created a chocolate board filled with candy, dried fruit, and nuts that can then be topped with an array of cheese and crackers.

Makes a chocolate board that is 10 x 15 x 1 inches (38 x 25.5 x 2.5 cm)

Plenty for 30 people.

CHOCOLATE BOARD

8 ¼ pounds (3700 g) milk chocolate

2.5 oz (70 g) dark chocolate

2.5 oz (70 g) white chocolate

⅓ cup (40 g / 1.4 oz) nuts, chopped

¼ cup (40 g / 1.4 oz) dried fruit

2 tablespoons (20 g / 0.7 oz) candied ginger (glace), chopped

½ cup (100 g / 3.5 oz) jelly beans

⅓ cup (70 g / 2.5 oz) soft toffees

2 Oreos (25 g / 0.9 oz)

Additional 2.5 oz (70 g) dark chocolate

Baking pan 10 x 15 x 1 inches (38 x 25.5 x 2.5 cm)

ASSEMBLY

2 different types of gourmet crackers

9 oz (260 g) Gouda cheese

14 oz (400 g) Jarlsberg cheese

9 oz (250 g) Edam cheese

7 oz (200 g) Camembert cheese

9 oz (250 g) Cheddar cheese

5 oz (150 g) Wensleydale cheese with cranberries

½ pound (225 g) grapes

1 fig

9 oz (250 g) strawberries

¼ cup (50 g / 1.8 oz) almonds

CHOCOLATE BOARD

Line the base of the baking pan or tin with nonstick baking paper. Ensure the baking paper is completely flat and doesn't cover the sides.

Temper the chocolate (see instructions on page 48). Mix half of the white chocolate with one tablespoon of milk chocolate, resulting in a light brown color. Drizzle the lined pan lengthwise with this light brown chocolate, then with the white chocolate and the dark chocolate. Run the drizzles along the full length of the pan, even spilling over the edges. Use a clean paintbrush to brush lightly down the length of the pan to smudge the chocolate; you are creating a "wood grain" effect, so make sure all the lines go in one direction.

Pour two thirds of the milk chocolate over the top and spread it out lengthwise. Do not swirl or spread it across the tin as this will ruin your wood grain. Sprinkle one half with candied ginger (glace ginger), dried fruit, and nuts and the other half with candies and crushed cookies. You can vary these fillings according to your taste. Pour over the remaining milk chocolate, then smooth out the top as best as you can. Drop the pan onto the counter a few times to get rid of any air bubbles. Place in the fridge for 1 hour to set.

Using a knife, scrape off any bumps on the chocolate so the board can sit flat. Flip the pan (tin) over and give it a gentle tap on the counter to tip out your chocolate board. Peel off the baking paper. Spread a very thin layer of melted dark chocolate over the top. Spread or brush it thin enough that you can see the various colors of the different chocolate underneath. Follow the edges of these different colors by running the tip of a sharp knife down the length of the board, making a slight indentation. Continue making lines down the board in a wood grain pattern. Place in the fridge for 10 minutes.

Using an offset spatula, gently scrape along the surface to smooth it out. Once you are happy with your wood grain look, fold a piece of paper towel, dip it into iced water, and quickly rub it back and forth along the surface. This will change the chocolate finish from a dull appearance to more like shiny, polished wood. You will need to replace the paper towel several times, continually dipping it into the iced water to keep it cold.

ASSEMBLY

When choosing your cheeses, look for a variety of shapes. Having one cheese that is wedge shaped, another round, and a third that is rectangular will make your board look more aesthetically pleasing.

Wash and dry the fresh fruit. Arrange the cheeses, fruit, crackers, and almonds on top of the board, then add a cheese knife. It's a good idea to have additional fruit and crackers set aside to restock the board as needed.

Video tutorial for this recipe can be found at howtocookthat.net/cookbook

Chocolate Cheese Board

LOCO COCONUT DESSERT

This dessert looks like a real coconut, but, in fact, it is a chocolate husk filled with delicious coconut mousse and fresh fruit. It incorporates a truly delicious treat from the Near East which can be ordered online if your hometown is lacking in international gourmet food shops. The servings are rather large, so it's a good idea to share one between two people.

Makes 4 coconut halves; enough dessert for 8 people.

CHOCOLATE HUSK

4 balloons

2 pounds (900 g) dark chocolate

1 ½ pounds (680 g) milk chocolate

7 oz (200 g) vanilla pashmak, also called pismaniye or Turkish fairy floss

COCONUT MOUSSE

11 gelatin sheets or 8 teaspoons powdered gelatin

A bowl of water if using gelatin sheets

½ cup (122 g / 4.3 oz) sugar

1 tablespoon vanilla or rum

1 ¾ cups (444 mL / 15 fl oz) coconut cream

4 ½ cups (1100 mL / 37.2 fl oz) heavy cream (35 percent fat)

ASSEMBLY

½ a fresh pineapple, peeled and diced

2 kiwi fruit, peeled and diced

2 cups (250 g / 8.8 oz) strawberries, halved

CHOCOLATE HUSK

Temper the dark chocolate (see page 48). Inflate the balloons to the size of a small coconut. Wash the outside of the balloon and dry with a paper towel. Dip the bottom half of each balloon into the dark chocolate to make a half sphere shape. Place onto nonstick baking paper to set; this will take about 20 minutes. (You won't be using all of the chocolate, but you will need this amount in the bowl to be able to dip the balloons.)

Temper the milk chocolate. Dip a dark chocolate-coated balloon into milk chocolate, then turn it upside down and sit it in a small bowl to hold it steady. While the chocolate is still very soft, drape long strands of pashmak across the balloon and down the sides, pressing it into the chocolate. Turn and repeat so the strands intersect at the center-top and all sides of the balloon have pashmak strands. Pour milk chocolate over the top; using a spatula, spread it out thinly so that you can still see the texture of the pashmak. Place in the fridge for 15 minutes. Repeat with the other balloons.

Make a small cut near the knot of the balloon and let the air out slowly. Remove the balloon. Use sharp scissors to trim any milk chocolate drips and pashmak to the level of the dark chocolate so it looks like half of a coconut husk.

COCONUT MOUSSE

Put the gelatin sheets into the water to soak. If using powdered gelatin, mix with 1 cup (250 mL / 8.5 fl oz) of the cream and set aside to soften.

Place the sugar, vanilla or rum, and coconut cream into a pan and heat until the sugar dissolves.

Squeeze the water out of the gelatin sheets and add them into the pan, stirring until they are melted. Set aside for 1 hour to cool to room temperature, but don't put the gelatin sheets in the fridge or they will set.

Whip the cream until you get stiff peaks, then fold through the coconut mixture. Fill each chocolate coconut husk with mousse and place them in the fridge for two hours to set.

Scoop out a shallow hole from the center of the mousse so that you have an even, white border around the edge just like a coconut. Warm a metal spoon in hot water and rub it along the inside edge so that it is nice and smooth.

Pile fresh fruit into the center of each dessert.

Video tutorial for this recipe can be found at howtocookthat.net/cookbook

IT'S NOT AN AVOCADO!

This dessert is a mind-bender for your guests. In order to eliminate the need for expensive custom molds, I came up with the idea of using the original avocado skin as a mold for a chocolate shell. This shell is filled with an avocado based citrus cream and a wonderful ganache "pip" or "pit."

Makes 6 avocado halves.

AVOCADO PITS (SEEDS)

3.5 oz (100 g) milk chocolate

2 ½ tablespoons (35 mL / 1.2 fl oz) heavy cream (35 percent fat)

6 balloons

AVOCADO SKINS

7.1 oz (200 g) dark chocolate

4 avocados

LIME AVOCADO CREAM

1 cup (250 mL / 8.5 fl oz) milk

2 teaspoons powdered gelatin

2 cups (430 g / 15.2 oz) green avocado flesh (the darker part nearer the avocado skin)

⅓ cup (70 g / 2.5 oz) sugar

3 teaspoons lime zest

2 tablespoons lime juice

ORANGE AVOCADO CREAM

1 teaspoon powdered gelatin

½ cup (125 mL / 4.2 fl oz) milk

1 cup (210 g / 7.4 oz) yellowish avocado flesh (the lighter flesh from nearer the center)

4 tablespoons (45 g / 1.6 oz) sugar

2 teaspoons orange zest

1 tablespoon orange juice

ALMOND PRALINE

1 cup (220 g / 7.8 oz) sugar

¼ cup (65 mL / 2.2 fl oz) water

1 cup (100 g / 3.5 oz) slivered almonds

ASSEMBLY

0.7 oz (20 g) dark chocolate

1 ½ teaspoons heavy cream (35 percent fat)

AVOCADO PITS (SEEDS)

Place the chocolate and cream into a bowl and heat on high in the microwave for one minute. Stir well, then return to the microwave for another 20 seconds and stir; repeat until the chocolate is melted. Whisk until the mixture is smooth.

Pipe your mixture into an uninflated balloon until it is about the size of an avocado pit. Tie the balloon and freeze overnight.

AVOCADO SKINS

Split each avocado in half lengthwise. Remove the pit and carefully spoon out the yellowy center part of the avocado flesh, leaving the green border behind. Put it into a bowl, cover, and refrigerate. Scrape out all the remaining green avocado flesh, place into a bowl, cover, and refrigerate. Keep 6 of your avocado skin halves, as you'll be using these as the mold for the desserts.

Melt the dark chocolate in the microwave on high for 1 minute and stir, microwave 30 seconds, stir again, repeating in 20-second bursts and stirring in between until melted. There is no need to temper this chocolate as it will be served chilled. Place 1½ tablespoons of the melted chocolate in an avocado skin, using the back of a spoon to spread it up the sides and all around the inside of your natural "mold." Repeat with the remaining avocado skins. Place in the fridge for 15 minutes to set.

LIME AVOCADO CREAM

Add 4 tablespoons of the milk to the gelatin and stir immediately. Set aside so the gelatin has time to absorb the moisture from the milk. Place the remaining milk in a blender or food processor with the green avocado flesh, sugar, lime zest, and lime juice. Blend until completely smooth and free of lumps. Heat the gelatin mixture in the microwave on high until it is melted, watching to make sure that it does not bubble over. Add it into the blender and mix together with the avocado mixture. Push your mixture though a fine sieve, using the back of a spoon to remove any flecks of lime zest.

ORANGE AVOCADO CREAM

Add 2 tablespoons of the milk to the gelatin and immediately stir. Set aside so the gelatin has time to absorb the moisture from the milk. Place the remaining milk in a blender or food processor with the yellow avocado flesh, sugar, orange zest, and orange juice. Blend until completely smooth and free of lumps. Heat the gelatin in the microwave until it is melted, watching to make sure that it does not bubble over. Add into the blender and mix together with the avocado mixture. Push this mixture though a fine sieve, using the back of a spoon to remove any flecks of orange zest.

ALMOND PRALINE

Line a baking sheet with nonstick baking paper and spread the slivered almonds out evenly on top. Put the sugar and water into a saucepan over high heat and stir until the sugar dissolves. Wash down the sides of the pan using a wet pastry brush to get rid of any sugar crystals on the sides. (If you don't do this, the candy may crystalize and become like fudge instead of being hard and clear.) Continue to boil unstirred over high heat until the bubbling slows and it starts to go golden. Now pour it over the slivered almonds. Do not touch this liquid, as it is hotter than boiling water. Set aside to cool, then smash it into small chunks and store in an airtight container.

ASSEMBLY

Place the dark chocolate and cream into a small bowl and microwave for 30 seconds on high. Stir until smooth, then set this dark chocolate ganache aside.

Take one shell out of the fridge at a time. Carefully peel the avocado skin off the chocolate. Pipe lime avocado cream around the edge and inside of each chocolate shell so it has a green border. Fill the center with your orange avocado cream. Level off the top.

Peel the balloon off each of the frozen balls of ganache and push each gently into the dessert in the position where you would expect to find an avocado pit. Using the back of a teaspoon, add a couple of small dabs of dark chocolate ganache to the base of the pit. Using a strip of baking paper, smear the ganache up and over the pit to give it some variation in color, just like a real avocado pit. Refrigerate and repeat for the rest of the desserts.

When you're ready to serve, place a spoonful of almond praline in the center of a plate and add a chocolate avocado dessert on top.

Video tutorial for this recipe can be found at howtocookthat.net/cookbook

It's Not an Avocado!

TRY NOT TO LAUGH DESSERT TUBES

There is something delightful about seeing your guests in fits of laughter as they eat one of these amazing dessert tubes...and then reach for another! I have served these tubes at both large corporate and small family events, and the results are always the same—lots of laughter at the embarrassing slurping sounds made by the tubes. They taste delicious, and it's great fun as people whip out their phones to film each other enjoying dessert. You will need to cut plexiglass tubing to size to make holders for this adventurous treat, so if you are looking for a DIY challenge, this fun dessert is for you!

Makes 22.

Allow 4 per person.

PAVLOVA DESSERT TUBES
22 x 1 fl oz (30 mL) tubes (see more information to the right)

STRAWBERRY JELLY (JELL-O)
1 box (85 g / 3 oz) strawberry jelly crystals (Jell-O)

1 ½ cups (400 mL / 13.5 fl oz) boiling water

MINI MERINGUES
1 egg white (30 g / 1 oz)

⅓ cup (50 g / 1.8 oz) sugar

1 teaspoon lemon juice or cream of tartar

ASSEMBLY
1 cup (120 g / 4.2 oz) strawberries, diced

⅔ cup (150 mL / 5.1 fl oz) heavy cream (35 percent fat), whipped

PAVLOVA DESSERT TUBES
I used plexiglass tubing with an inside diameter of 20 mm (¾ inch), then cut it with a saw into 15 cm (6 inch) lengths and sanded the top and base to make them smooth. They are reusable as well as food and dishwasher safe.

MINI MERINGUES
Preheat the oven to 150°C (302°F). Whip together the egg white, sugar, and lemon juice at high speed for 5 minutes until they form stiff peaks. Put the mixture into a piping bag or Ziploc bag with the corner cut off, then pipe tiny meringues onto nonstick baking paper. Bake for 15–20 minutes or until crisp.

Allow to cool and store in an airtight container until needed.

STRAWBERRY JELLY (JELL-O)
Put the jelly crystals (Jell-O mix) into a bowl and pour over the boiling water. Stir until the sugar and gelatin are dissolved.

Place your dessert tubes upright in a small container. It's best if the tubes fit tightly to the edge of the container so they stay upright. Pour the strawberry jelly (Jell-O) into the container and place it in the fridge for at least 2 hours to set.

ASSEMBLY
Wash, hull, and finely dice the strawberries. Pipe some whipped cream into each dessert tube on top of the strawberry jelly (Jell-O) until it reaches the halfway point. Add in mini meringues, filling each tube up to the three-quarter mark, and then top with finely diced strawberries.

Serve within 2 hours of adding the meringues. Lift each tube out of the strawberry jelly (Jell-O), and wipe the outside of the tube clean using a paper towel. Place the dessert tubes upright in a container. Serve to the table with a bowl of hot water. Instruct your guests to dip the jelly (Jell-O) end of the tube into the hot water for 3–5 seconds to slightly loosen it from the tube, then suck on the top end of the tube to get the dessert. You will need a container handy to collect empty tubes.

Makes 22.

Allow 4 per person.

ROOT BEER FLOAT DESSERT TUBES

22 x 1 fl oz (30 mL) tubes (see more
  information to the left)

ROOT BEER GEL

1 ½ cups (400 mL / 13.5 fl oz) root
  beer

2 teaspoons powdered gelatin

THIN CUSTARD

2 tablespoons (20 g / 0.7 oz) sugar

2 egg yolks (30 g / 1 oz)

⅔ cup (183 mL / 6.2 fl oz) heavy cream
  (35 percent fat)

1 teaspoon vanilla extract

FIZZY SHERBET POWDER

¾ cups (95 g / 3.35 oz) icing sugar or
  powdered sugar

3 teaspoons citric acid

1 ½ teaspoons baking soda
  (bi-carb soda)

ASSEMBLY

¾ cup (100 g / 3.5 oz) Sherbet
  (see above)

⅔ cup (150 mL / 5.1 fl oz) heavy cream
  (35 percent fat), whipped

ROOT BEER FLOAT DESSERT TUBES

ROOT BEER GEL

Put the gelatin into a large bowl and stir in ½ cup of root beer. Leave to stand for 5 minutes so the gelatin can soften. Heat in the microwave on high until it starts to bubble and the gelatin is melted. Stir in the rest of the root beer. Place the tubes upright in a container. Pour the root beer gel mixture into the container and place in the fridge for at least 2 hours to set.

THIN CUSTARD

Whisk together the sugar, egg yolks, cream, and vanilla in a pan. Stir continuously over high heat until it thickens slightly and just begins to boil. Immediately remove from the heat and tip into a bowl to cool.

FIZZY SHERBET POWDER

This fizzy sherbet powder is very different to the frozen dessert familiar to many—this is a flavored powdered sugar that fizzes when you eat it. You can use store-bought sherbet, but if it is not available where you live, it is easy to make. Sift the icing sugar, citric acid, and baking soda (bi-carb soda) into a bowl. Stir well and store in an airtight container until needed.

ASSEMBLY

For each tube, pipe the cooled custard on top of the root beer gel until it reaches the halfway point. About 30 minutes before you are ready to serve, use a funnel to add 1½ teaspoons of sherbet powder to each tube (and if you don't have a funnel, just use a cone made from paper). Pipe some whipped cream on top of each one. Lift each tube out of the gel and wipe the outside clean using a paper towel, then place upright in a container. Serve to the table with a bowl of hot water and instruct guests to dip the gel end of the tube into the hot water for 3-5 seconds. Finally, enjoy the laughter as your guests suck on the tubes to get the dessert. You will need a container handy to collect empty tubes.

Video tutorial for this recipe can be found at howtocookthat.net/cookbook

Try Not to Laugh Dessert Tubes

3D GELATINA SPIDERS & FLOWERS

Arachnophobia, the fear of spiders, affects nearly a third of all people. Add to that trypanophobia, the fear of needles, and this is one scary recipe! The flowers and spiders are made by injecting a milk-based gelatin mixture into a clear sweet gelatina.

Gelatin flowers have their origins in Mexico, where they are called gelatina floral. The spiders originated in my kitchen after my boys were not overly impressed with the pretty flowers.

Makes one large 1.25 L (0.33 gal) gelatina or 10 x 125 mL (4.2 fl oz) individual ones.

CLEAR GELATINA

4 tablespoons (56 g / 2 oz) powdered gelatin

1 cup (250 mL / 8.45 fl oz) cold water

4 cups (1 litre / 1 quart) water

1 ⅓ (300 g / 10.6 oz) cup sugar

¼ teaspoon citric acid (or other uncolored flavoring)

MILK-BASED GELATINA

2 tablespoons (20 g / 0.7 oz) gelatin

½ cup (125 mL / 4 fl oz) water

One 14 oz (395 g) can sweetened condensed milk

1 cup (250 mL / 8.4 fl oz) milk

Pink, blue, and yellow food color

0.7 oz (20 g) dark chocolate, melted

DESIGNS

Five 19G (38 mm / 1.5 inch) hypodermic needles with luer lock

Five 0.34 fl oz (10 mL) luer lock syringes (one per color)

Flexible plastic

Small plastic toy spiders

CLEAR GELATINA

Quickly mix together the gelatin with 1 cup of cold water. Set it aside until the gelatin has absorbed the water.

Place the quart (1 litre) of water, sugar, and citric acid into a saucepan and heat until the sugar dissolves. Add the gelatin and stir until it is melted. Pour into smooth-bottomed clear plastic or glass containers and place in the fridge to set.

MILK-BASED GELATINA

Mix together the gelatin and cold water and leave to one side.

Heat the milk and the sweetened condensed milk in a saucepan until it just starts to boil. Watch to make sure it does not boil over. Remove it from the heat, add the gelatin, and stir until it is melted. Split into 5 small bowls. Leave one bowl plain and color three of the others pink, blue, and yellow. Add the melted dark chocolate to the fifth bowl and stir through. You can make combinations or different strengths of colors as needed. If the any of the mixtures set before you are ready to use them, you can remelt it in the microwave, but watch carefully so it doesn't bubble up and spill over.

DESIGNS

Large syringes can be purchased from veterinary supply stores or online. Purchase luer lock needles since they twist and lock into place instead of pushing on, which is important because our mixture is quite thick. To fill the syringes with milk-based gelatina, take the needle off the syringe, put the end of the syringe into the liquid, and pull the plunger back. Wipe the end clean and twist the needle back on. (If the gelatina sets in the syringe while you are working, take off the metal needle and put the needle into boiling water to clean. Meanwhile, place the plastic syringe full of gelatina into the microwave for 3-second bursts until the gelatina is liquid again. Finally, put the needle back onto the syringe and squeeze out a little of the mixture to get rid on any unwanted water.)

FLOWERS

Firm but flexible plastic can be found in lots of food packaging, such as empty yogurt containers or milk bottles. Cut out four or more rectangles about 2 x ½ inches (5 x 1.5 cm) from the plastic. Cut one end of the rectangle to be the shape of the top of a flower petal. Depending on the flower that you want to make, this shape may be rounded like a rose petal or skinny and come together in a point at the top for a water lily petal.

(A thin plastic or metal spoon can also be useful when making petals.) You can actually buy shaped metal needle accessories to make floral gelatinas, but, unless you're planning to make hundreds of them, these homemade plastic ones work perfectly.

Push the shaped plastic into the clear gelatina where you want the petal to be. Leave it inserted, then push it down slightly using the tip of the needle so that you have a little gap between the plastic and the gelatina. Inject the milk gelatina into this gap. Remove the plastic; then, using a spoon, wipe off any excess milk gelatina sitting on top. Turn the gelatina upside down to see what the petal looks like and where to position the next one. If you space out the insertion point of the plastic too much, it will look like the petals are not attached to each other. To avoid this, start each petal close to an existing one and simply adjust the angle of insertion to make petals that are further out. When you have finished making all the petals, drip some extra color on the back of the gelatina in the same color as your flower. This fills in any gaps that you may have between the petals.

To make jagged petals like those on a carnation, you do not need to use any plastic. Insert the needle and squeeze out some milk gelatina. Repeatedly pull the needle a tiny way out and back in while at the same time moving the needle tip across inside the gelatina. It will look best if you angle the needle so that you keep the insertion point still but move the needle tip across to make jagged fan-shaped petals. Once you have done all the petals, drip some extra color on the back. Experiment using two different colors, such as white petals and pink drips. Use your finger to gently press up and down on the drips to encourage some of the mixture into the gaps, resulting in a two-toned petal.

To make a rose, use different sized metal spoons for the petal indents. Use the smallest spoons at the center, progressing out to larger ones at the edge.

Once the petals have set, turn them upside down so you can see the flower. Using yellow or white milk gelatina, push the needle straight in at the center, inject a tiny bit of yellow, and pull it straight out. This will make the filaments that are in the middle of most flowers. Make sure you do not go through any of your petals.

Allow the flowers to set in the fridge for about ten minutes before pouring a thin layer of colored milk gelatina over the back. My favorite is a mixture of light and deep blue, but you could try dark brown for a more dramatic look.

SPIDERS

You will need to make this before you set the clear gelatina. If it is already set, then you can melt it in the microwave or on the stovetop. Take a toy plastic spider and cut the legs off so that you are left with only the head and abdomen. (You can carve this shape out of a carrot if you do not have a toy spider.) Poke a tooth pick through a piece of sticky tape and into the tummy side of the body. Put the tape across the top of the container so that the back of the spider is sitting in the clear gelatina liquid all the way up to, but not covering, the tummy. Put it in the fridge.

Once it is set, run the tip of a clean needle around the very top edge of the toy spider to loosen it and remove it from the gelatina. Make brown milk gelatina by adding in some melted dark chocolate. You can vary the amount of chocolate to make different shades. Your spiders will look more realistic if there is some variation in the body color. For example, using your needle, you could paint some brown stripes down the abdomen, then take the needle off the end and use the syringe to fill the spider body with a different shade of brown. Allow that to set in the fridge.

For the legs, insert the needle at the base on one side of the head, then squeeze a tiny bit of brown and pull it straight out. A spider has four legs on each side of the head section (cephalothorax) and none from the abdomen. Look at a picture of a spider to check the angle of its legs. Now insert the needle where the end of the leg would be sitting on the ground, angling it into the gelatina to join up with the top of the leg section. This way, you end up with legs that go up from the body and then bend back down to the floor. Using a spoon, scrape off any excess brown mixture from the bottom. You can pour on a different color for the base, or else leave it clear so it looks like a real spider specimen.

Video tutorial for this recipe can be found at howtocookthat.net/cookbook

CANDY SUGAR BALLOON BOWLS

I love experimenting in the kitchen, developing fresh and new ideas. When I created this recipe a few years ago, there were no blog posts or online videos about Balloon Sugar Bowls. They simply didn't exist yet. After experimenting with different materials to find one that wouldn't melt when coated with scalding candy, I finally discovered a technique that worked. The resulting sugar bowls turned out more beautiful and amazing than I'd imagined! I just had to share it with the world.

SUGAR BOWLS

1 ⅓ cups (300 g / 10.6 oz) sugar

½ cup (200 g / 7 oz) glucose syrup or light corn syrup

⅓ cup (75 mL / 2.5 fl oz) water

Clear flavoring (optional)

Liquid food colors (red, blue, yellow)

EQUIPMENT

Candy thermometer

Helium quality balloons

Fill your helium quality balloons with water to make them the desired size. Remove any remaining air by holding it upright and letting a little of the water squirt out the top. Then tie the balloon and place it upside down on a small bowl resting on some baking paper. Dry the balloon with paper towel and then rub it with a little cooking oil.

Mix the sugar, water, and glucose syrup together in a saucepan. Place over high heat and stir until the sugar is dissolved. Wash down the sides of the pan, using a wet pastry brush to remove any sugar crystals from the sides. Add a candy thermometer to the side of the pan and heat the syrup without stirring until it reaches 150°C (300°F). Remove from the heat, then stir in your desired flavor and add drops of color. If you are using multiple colors, do not stir, just allow them to mingle as you pour.

Wait until the bubbles have subsided, then slowly pour the mixture over your water-filled balloons, allowing the excess to drip down onto the baking paper. Be careful, this mixture is very hot.

Leave to cool completely (approximately 15 minutes). Holding a balloon over the sink, make a small cut in the balloon near the knot and let it empty while you hold the sugar bowl. Repeat with each balloon.

Store in an airtight container at room temperature until ready to use. Hard sugar candy absorbs moisture from the air, so if you leave it exposed, it will become sticky. Serve filled with ice cream and fruit or any dessert of your choosing.

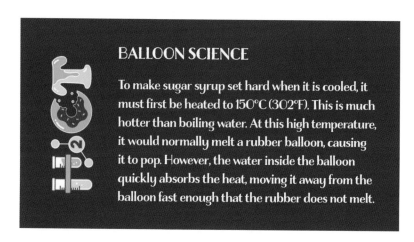

BALLOON SCIENCE

To make sugar syrup set hard when it is cooled, it must first be heated to 150°C (302°F). This is much hotter than boiling water. At this high temperature, it would normally melt a rubber balloon, causing it to pop. However, the water inside the balloon quickly absorbs the heat, moving it away from the balloon fast enough that the rubber does not melt.

Video tutorial for this recipe can be found at howtocookthat.net/cookbook

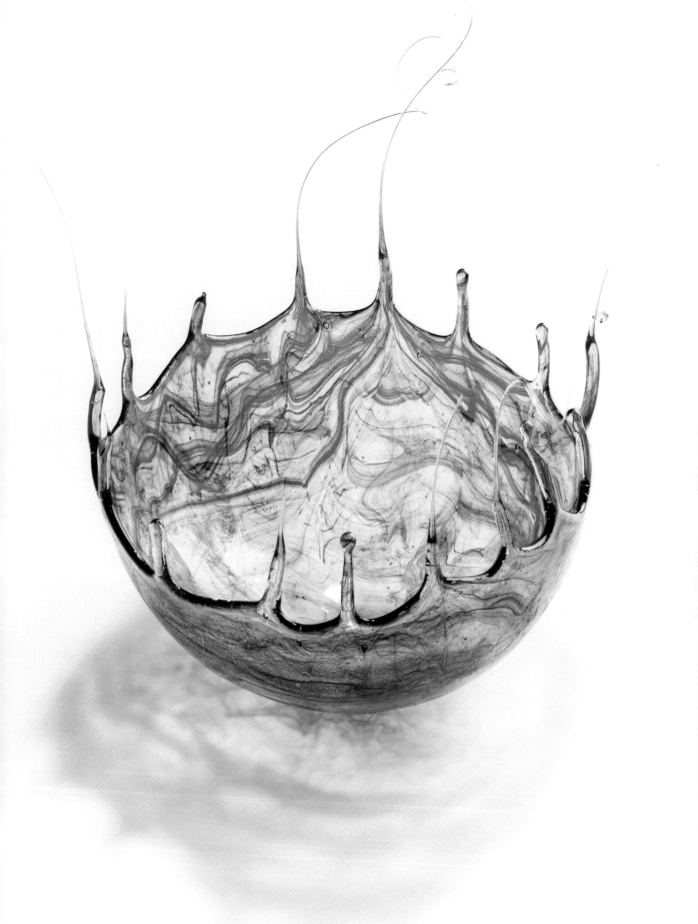

APPLE-SHAPED DESSERT

My challenge with this recipe was to find a way to shape the creamy vanilla mousse and cinnamon apple chunks so that it looked like a real apple without using expensive molds. It looks wonderful and tastes lovely too—a real restaurant quality dessert in your own home.

Makes 4 apples.

APPLE CENTER

3 apples, peeled and finely diced

½ cup (120 g / 4.2 oz) apple puree

1 teaspoon vanilla extract

¼ teaspoon cinnamon

4 balloons washed

VANILLA MOUSSE

2 cups (500 mL / 17 fl oz) milk

2 ½ tablespoons (35 g / 1.2 oz) powdered gelatin

1 tablespoon vanilla

6 egg yolks (90 g / 3.2 oz)

7 tablespoons (50 g / 1.8 oz) corn flour or cornstarch

⅓ cup (80 g / 2.8 oz) sugar

3 ¼ cups (800 mL / 27 fl oz) heavy cream (35 percent fat)

Empty small plastic soda bottle

APPLE STEMS

1.8 oz (50 g) dark chocolate

Marsala or other similar fortified wine with 15–20 percent alcohol

RED GLAZE

1 cup water (250 mL / 8.4 fl oz)

2 tablespoons powdered gelatin

1 ⅓ cups (300 g / 10.6 oz) caster sugar or superfine sugar

⅔ cup (220 g / 7.8 oz) sweetened condensed milk

10.6 oz (300 g) white chocolate

Red gel food coloring

APPLE CENTER

Combine the diced apple with the apple puree, vanilla, and cinnamon. Place a tablespoon of this mixture into each balloon and shape them into balls. Do not tie the balloons but place them in the freezer for several hours.

VANILLA MOUSSE

Stir a small amount of the milk into the gelatin until you have a runny paste, then leave to one side. Put the remaining milk into a pan with the vanilla.

In a bowl, whisk the egg yolks, sugar, and corn flour together. Once smooth, add into the pan.

Place over high heat, stirring constantly until it thickens. Keep stirring over a medium heat for another minute to cook the corn flour. Remove from the stove and add the softened gelatin, stirring until it melts. Mix in the cream, then leave to cool to room temperature.

Whip on high speed until it is airy and slightly thickened. Pour into a clean soda bottle (a piping bag or funnel will make this easier). Working quickly before the mousse sets, take one of your balloons out of the freezer and inflate it to a size that is a little larger than an apple. Twist the neck to stop it deflating, and stretch the neck of the balloon over the top of the soda bottle while keeping it closed. Allow the balloon to untwist; then, holding the balloon onto the neck of the bottle, tip the bottle and squeeze, pouring in enough mousse to make a good-sized apple. Twist the neck of the balloon to seal it again, remove from the bottle, and tie in a knot. Use your fingers to position the frozen apple ball in the center of the mousse and return to the freezer for 3 hours.

APPLE STEMS

Place a small bowl of Marsala in the freezer and leave to chill for several hours.

Melt some chocolate in the microwave on high, then pour it into a piping bag or Ziploc bag with a small corner cut off. Pipe lines of chocolate into the Marsala; once set, remove them with a fork and drain on a paper towel. Store in the fridge until you are ready to use them.

If you prefer, you can pipe stems of chocolate onto foil, but they will be flat on one side if you use this method.

RED GLAZE

Stir a small amount of the water in with the gelatin to form a runny paste and set aside.

Place the rest of the water, sugar, and sweetened condensed milk into a heatproof bowl. Microwave on high for 1 minute and stir. Then repeat in bursts of 30 seconds, stirring each time until the sugar is dissolved.

Add the softened gelatin and stir through until it is melted. Add the white chocolate and leave to stand for a few minutes. Stir the now-melted white chocolate through the mixture, then add red food coloring to give a bright color.

Before using, let the glaze cool to room temperature, but do not refrigerate or it will set. If it does set before you are ready, simply microwave half of the mixture to remelt it, then stir it back into the other half to cool it again.

You need this amount of glaze so that you can dip the apples in it. After they are dipped, you will have leftover glaze that can be frozen for several months if necessary.

ASSEMBLY

Cut the top off the balloon and peel it back. Use a knife to cut a dip in the top of the frozen ball so it looks like an apple. Flatten the base slightly so it sits on a plate without tipping over.

Stick a skewer in the top. Paint a couple of stripes with red food coloring. and then dip the apple into the glaze. Allow the excess to drip off and place the apple onto the serving plate. Add the chocolate stem to the top. Repeat for each balloon. Defrost in the fridge for at least 3 hours before serving.

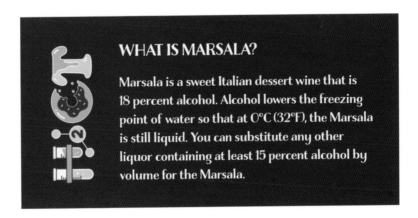

WHAT IS MARSALA?

Marsala is a sweet Italian dessert wine that is 18 percent alcohol. Alcohol lowers the freezing point of water so that at 0°C (32°F), the Marsala is still liquid. You can substitute any other liquor containing at least 15 percent alcohol by volume for the Marsala.

Video tutorial for this recipe can be found at howtocookthat.net/cookbook

Apple-Shaped Dessert

EMOJI SURPRISE INSIDE DESSERT

Slice this dessert open at the table to reveal the heart eyes emoji on every slice. After your guests have finished snapping photos of their dessert, the finale will be the exclamations that it tastes "oh so good."

10 slices.

RASPBERRY CRÉMEUX

1 tablespoon (14 g / 0.5 oz) powdered gelatin

3 tablespoons (45 mL / 1.5 fl oz) water

¼ cup (55 g / 1.9 oz) sugar

7 egg yolks (105 g / 3.7 oz)

17.6 oz (500 g) white chocolate

1 ¾ cups (450 mL / 15.2 fl oz) heavy cream (35 percent fat)

½ cup (75 g / 2.6 oz) raspberries

Red food coloring

Heart-shaped cookie cutter

SMILEY MOUTH

1 ½ teaspoon powdered gelatin

2 tablespoons (30 mL / 1 fl oz) water

8.8 oz (250 g) milk chocolate

1 cup (275 mL / 9.3 fl oz) heavy cream (35 percent fat)

3 egg yolks (45 g / 1.6 oz)

2 tablespoons (27 g / 0.9 oz) sugar

Cylinder-shaped container with lid, measuring as close as possible to 3.6 inches (9.2 cm) in diameter and 6.9 inches (17.5 cm) tall

ASSEMBLY

Cylindrical container 5 inches (13 cm) in diameter, 6 inches (16 cm) tall, i.e., wider than the mouth cylinder

WHITE CHOCOLATE MOUSSE

3 tablespoons (42 g / 1.5 oz) powdered gelatin

¾ cup (185 mL / 6 fl oz) water

9 egg yolks (135 g / 4.8 oz)

¼ cup (30 g / 1.1 oz) corn flour (cornstarch)

½ cup (120 g / 4.2 oz) sugar

3 ⅔ cups (900 mL / 30.4 fl oz) heavy cream (35 percent fat)

RASPBERRY CRÉMEUX

Line a 10 x 15 inch (25 x 38 cm) baking pan with aluminum foil. Put the water and gelatin into a bowl and immediately stir together.

In a separate bowl, add the sugar to the egg yolks and whisk together. Break the chocolate into a different bowl and place a sieve over the top.

Heat the cream and raspberries in a saucepan until they just start to boil, watching carefully so it does not boil over. Pour half a cup of the hot cream and raspberries into the egg yolk mixture and whisk until combined. Pour this egg yolk mixture into the pan with the rest of the cream, whisking as you do. Heat for just 60 seconds, then immediately remove from the heat (as overheating will cause it to split and go lumpy). Add in the gelatin and stir until melted.

Pour the mixture through the sieve onto the chocolate. Push it through the sieve using the back of a spoon until only the raspberry seeds are left behind, then discard them. Wait for a couple of minutes, then whisk the raspberry chocolate mixture until smooth. Add red food coloring and mix well. Pour into the lined baking pan and freeze for at least 3 hours.

SMILEY MOUTH

Add the gelatin to the water and quickly stir it through so you don't have any lumps. Break the chocolate into pieces and set aside in a different large bowl.

In a separate bowl, whisk together the sugar and the egg yolks. Place the cream into the saucepan and heat until it just starts to boil. Pour half a cup of the hot cream into the egg yolks and whisk well together. Add this egg yolk mixture into the pan with the rest of the cream, whisking as you do so.

Return it to the heat for one minute only or until it reaches 185°C (85°F). Immediately remove it from the heat and add the gelatin. Stir until it melts, then pour the mixture over your chocolate. Wait two minutes; then stir until smooth.

Half fill a cylinder container with the mixture. Screw the lid on, then tip the container onto its side to make the smiley mouth shape. Place in the freezer for at least 3 hours.

ASSEMBLY

Remove the smiley mouth from the container and add a skewer in the center of one end to hold it (the skewer does not need to go the whole way through). If you are having trouble getting it out, run the outside of the container under hot water to make it easier.

Cut as many hearts as possible from the frozen pan of red crémeux. Take the offcuts (scraps) and melt them in the microwave.

1 ¼ cups (300 mL / 10.1 fl oz)
    additional heavy cream
    (35 percent fat)
13.8 oz (390 g) white chocolate
1 ½ teaspoons vanilla
Yellow food coloring

ORANGE GLAZE

¾ cup (200 mL / 6 fl oz) orange juice
4 teaspoons (56 g / 2 oz) gelatin
¼ cup (25 g / 0.9 oz) corn flour
    (cornstarch)
½ cup (150 g / 5.3 oz) glucose syrup or
    light corn syrup
1 ¼ cups (280 g / 9.9 oz) sugar
1 tablespoon water
1 ⅓ cups (350 g / 12.4 oz) heavy cream
    (35 percent fat)
8.1 oz (230 g) white chocolate
Orange food coloring

CHOCOLATE DECORATION

5.3 oz (150 g) white chocolate
Orange oil-based food coloring or
    powdered food coloring

Use the melted crémeux to "glue" together your hearts into two tall stacks, one for each eye. Once it reaches the height of your container, add a skewer down the center.

Place the eyes and mouth in position in a cylindrical container with the skewers sticking out above the top of the container. Use tape to secure the skewers into place so the eyes and mouth stay vertical and do not lean. Return to the freezer while you make the mousse.

WHITE CHOCOLATE MOUSSE

Mix together the gelatin and water and leave to soften. In another bowl, whisk together the egg yolks, corn flour, and sugar.

Place the 3⅔ cups (900 mL / 30.4 fl oz) of cream into a pan and heat it until it just starts to boil. Whisk half a cup of hot cream into the egg yolks. Add the warm egg yolk mixture back into the pan with the rest of the cream. Stir over the heat for a minute or until it thickens slightly. Remove from the heat, add in the gelatin, and stir until it is melted. Add the white chocolate; leave it for two minutes and then whisk together. Add yellow food coloring until you have a bright emoji color. Leave to cool to room temperature.

Whip the remaining cream and vanilla to soft peaks. Fold into the yellow mousse. Take the container with the eyes and mouth out of the freezer. The hearts and smile should by now be frozen to the base so you can remove the tape. Add a sheet of acetate (clear plastic) around the inside of the cylinder to make it easier to get it out later. Pour in the mousse, filling it right up to the top of the container. Gently bang it on the counter to remove any large air bubbles. Freeze for at least 3 hours.

ORANGE GLAZE

Add three tablespoons of orange juice to the gelatin and quickly stir it through. In a separate bowl combine two tablespoons of the orange juice with the corn flour, making sure there are no lumps.

Put the glucose syrup, sugar, and water into a pan and stir over high heat until the sugar is dissolved and looks clear. Add the corn flour mixture and the rest of the orange juice to the pan and stir until the mixture starts to boil. Remove from the heat and add your gelatin, stirring until melted. Tip in the chocolate and leave for a couple of minutes.

Stir in the now-melted chocolate. Add the cream and orange food coloring and mix well. Leave the glaze to cool to room temperature. If your glaze sets before you are ready to use it, you'll need to remelt it in the microwave (microwave on high 30 seconds and stir, repeating as necessary), then cool it to room temperature again.

Remove the dessert from the freezer and place the base of the container in warm water until it is loosened. Pull it out of the container and remove the acetate. Place two drinking glasses in a baking pan and balance the dessert across the top. Now you can spoon generous scoops of glaze over the top. It is important that the glaze is at room temperature. If it's too hot, it will melt a layer of the dessert and slide off. And if it's too cold, it won't flow over the dessert.

Once the first layer is set, give it a second coat of glaze. Carefully lift the dessert off and place it onto a serving platter. If necessary, to stop it rolling, add some cookie crumbs along each side. Then leave it in the fridge to defrost.

CHOCOLATE DECORATION

Melt the chocolate in the microwave for 60 seconds on high, then stir, microwave for another 30 seconds, stir, and then repeat in 30-second bursts, stirring each time until melted. Take a small amount of the chocolate and color it orange. You cannot use gel or liquid color for this as it will seize the chocolate.

Spread some of the white chocolate onto baking paper in a circle, about the same size as the end of the dessert. Pipe a spiral of orange chocolate on top. If you have a cake turntable, then you can easily pipe the spiral by spinning the turntable while slowly moving the piping bag from the center toward the outside.

Lift the baking paper and tap it on the counter to smooth. Once it is dry to the touch, but not yet firm, place a small round bowl over the top and cut around it to make a neat circle. Remove the bowl, and place a sheet of baking paper with a heavy book on top to keep the chocolate flat.

Once your dessert has defrosted, you can pull out the skewers. Add the chocolate circles over each end. Slice at the table to surprise your guests with the heart emoji smiley face on every serving.

Video tutorial for this recipe can be found at howtocookthat.net/cookbook

LIQUID CHOCOLATE SPHERICALS

Sphericals are great for cocktail parties, providing a fun explosion of flavor in your mouth. As with most baking, making these sphericals requires a chemical reaction to occur. However, in this case, you have to get the mix perfect. If there is too much acid, fat, or alcohol in the liquid, it simply won't work. The limited fat in the recipe was a puzzle in trying to develop a great-tasting chocolate spherical. After persevering through many failed experiments, I came up with one that works and is delicious, too.

ALGINATE BATH
¼ gallon (1 litre) warm water
1 teaspoon (5 g / 0.2 oz) sodium alginate

LIQUID CHOCOLATE
3.5 oz (100 g) dark chocolate
¾ cup (200 mL / 7 fl oz) heavy cream (35 percent fat)
1 tablespoon (20 g / 0.7 oz) caster sugar or superfine sugar
1 tablespoon (6 g / 0.2 oz) grated fresh ginger (optional)
1 teaspoon (3.2 g / 0.1 oz) food-grade Calcium Lactate powder

ALGINATE BATH
Place the warm water in a blender and turn it on low. While it is running, add in the sodium alginate and blend until well combined. Pour into a clean bowl, cover, and leave overnight for the bubbles to come the surface. Alginate gels in the presence of calcium, so if you live somewhere where there is a lot of calcium in the tap water (known as hard water), you will need to use bottled water for this.

LIQUID CHOCOLATE
Chop the chocolate and place into a bowl with a sieve over the top.

In a pan, combine the cream, ginger, sugar, and Calcium Lactate powder. Bring to a boil, then remove from the heat. Let it sit for 10 minutes to allow the ginger flavor to infuse into the cream. Reheat to a boil again, then pour through the sieve onto the chocolate. Leave for 2 minutes, then whisk the now-melted chocolate into the cream.

Place the mixture into a spherical ice cube tray in the freezer, or you could let it freeze in the bowl and then use a melon baller to get round scoops of mixture.

Drop the balls of frozen chocolate mixture into the alginate bath. Gently stir. The calcium in the chocolate mixture causes the alginate to gel, encapsulating the ball. Leave in bath for 1–2 minutes. The longer you leave it, the thicker the membrane will be. Only do a couple at a time as the balls will fuse together if they touch. Remove and place in bowl of warm water. Serve on a spoon. Flat-bottomed Chinese soupspoons are a great presentation choice.

Video tutorial for this recipe can be found at howtocookthat.net/cookbook

WHAT IS ALGINATE?

Alginate is found naturally in brown seaweed or algae. In contrast to gelatin, which only gels when cold, alginate gels if calcium is present. The gel it forms is heat-stable, meaning that you can heat these sphericals and the gel layer will not melt. You have probably eaten alginate before as it is commonly used as a stabilizer or thickener in low-fat ice cream, salad dressing, and yogurt.

SHOW-OFF
PASTRIES

SHOW-OFF PASTRIES

Egyptians, Greeks, and Romans are credited with inventing the earliest pastries, although they were very different from what we know today. The Romans made a paste from flour, water, and oil to encase meat while cooking and prevent moisture loss. The cooked paste was then discarded. It wasn't until much later, when European cooks swapped the oil for butter, that the pastry was eaten.

There are four basic types of pastry:

FILO PASTRY

Filo or phyllo pastry is made with very little fat. It comes in paper-thin sheets that are quite fragile and can rip easily. Several sheets of filo are often used together to create a flaky casing for fillings. Or it can be layered up with butter, cinnamon, and nuts before being drizzled in sweet honey syrup to make baklava.

SWEET SHORT CRUST PASTRY

This is the most common dessert pastry. It is crumbly, or "short," similar to shortbread. It's made by rubbing butter into flour before adding sugar and enough liquid to bind it together. It resists soaking up fluids, making it perfect for fruit pies, custard tarts, or other dishes.

It is important not to overwork the pastry once you have added the liquid, as this causes the gluten in the flour to develop, making the dough elastic and stretchy. You want elasticity in bread, but not in pastry, as it will shrink and become tough when baked. This can also happen if you have a high ratio of liquid to fat in your pastry recipe.

You can experiment with altering the recipe for short crust pastry. For example, substituting an equal volume of egg for some of the water in a recipe provides a richer flavor and more protein for structure. Swapping out some of the flour for ground nuts increases flavor and reduces the amount of gluten, making the pastry slightly more crumbly when baked. You can also decrease the sugar, or leave it out altogether, to offset a sweet filling.

CHOUX PASTRY

Choux pastry is made from flour, water, butter, and eggs. As batter, it is thick, gooey, and can be piped. When it is baked, the water evaporates to create steam, which is trapped inside the dough. This causes the dough to puff into a hollow centered pillow with a crisp exterior. The middle is typically filled with custard or cream. You will be familiar with choux pastry in a chocolate éclair, profiterole, or croquembouche (see page 138).

PUFF PASTRY

Claude Gelee invented puff pastry in 1645 while trying to make a rolled butter cake for his ill father. Today, it is made by laminating fat (usually butter) and pastry dough into very thin layers. When baked, the steam is trapped between the dough layers, causing the dough to puff up into thin crispy layers. You can make your own puff pastry at home, but it is time-consuming as the dough needs to chill in the fridge between stages of rolling. Store-bought versions are convenient; and, unless you are an experienced pastry chef, they usually have superior lamination than can be achieved at home.

CHOCOLATE RASPBERRY TART

This chocolate raspberry tart is neat, tidy, simple, and dare I say it...perfect. It is beautiful to look at and follows through on its visual promise with gorgeous taste and texture.

One 8-inch (20 cm) round tart, yielding 6-8 slices.

PASTRY

½ cup (125 g / 4.4 oz) butter

1 ¼ cups (200 g / 7 oz) plain or all-purpose flour

¼ cup (50 g / 1.8 oz) sugar

1 egg (45 g / 1.6 oz)

½ teaspoon vanilla

Ceramic baking weights or you can use uncooked rice or dried beans

8-inch (20 cm) loose-based baking pan (a springform pan or one with a removable base)

CHOCOLATE FILLING

7 oz (200 g) dark chocolate

7 oz (200 g) milk chocolate

5 egg yolks (85 g / 3 oz)

3 tablespoons (40 g / 1.4 oz) caster sugar or superfine sugar

1 cup (250 mL / 8.4 fl oz) heavy cream (35 percent fat)

¾ cup (210 mL / 7 fl oz) milk

DECORATION

1 ⅔ cup (250 g / 8.8 oz) fresh raspberries

5.3 oz (150 g) dark chocolate, tempered

Square notched cake comb

Sheet of acetate or bendy plastic

PASTRY

Preheat the oven to 180°C (350°F).

Using your thumb and fingers, rub the butter into the flour; keep going until it resembles breadcrumbs. Stir in the sugar. Lightly whisk the egg and vanilla and stir into the flour mixture.

Squeeze the mixture together to form a ball, but do not knead the pastry dough. Place it onto some plastic wrap and use the palm of your hand to flatten it down into a disc shape. Put another sheet of plastic wrap over the top and roll it out to make a circle that is slightly bigger than your base.

Remove the loose base from your tin and line it with baking paper. Peel the top sheet of plastic wrap off the pastry. Lift the pastry, and with the plastic wrap still underneath to support it, flip it over onto the base. Peel off the plastic, trim around the edge, and then return the sides of the loose-based pan into place.

Roll the remaining pastry into a snake and roll it out between two sheets of plastic wrap. Peel off the top plastic. Using a ruler and a sharp pizza cutter, cut 1 inch (2.5 cm) strips of pastry, cutting right through the bottom plastic wrap. Pick up the strip with the plastic still underneath it and gently press the pastry around the edges of the tin so that it is just touching the base. Smooth out the pastry and remove the plastic wrap. Repeat with another strip until you have gone the whole way around the tart.

Line with baking paper and add ceramic baking weights on top of the paper. Bake in the oven for 10 minutes, then carefully remove the hot baking weights and paper. Do not tip the pastry shell to get the weights out or the pastry may fall out; try using a spoon instead. Return to the oven for 25–30 minutes or until it is crisp and golden brown. Set aside to cool.

CHOCOLATE FILLING

Break the chocolate into pieces and place in a bowl with a fine sieve sitting over the top. Set aside. Whisk together the sugar and egg yolks until pale. In a saucepan, heat the cream and milk until they just start to boil. Remove from the heat. Whisk about ¼ cup of the hot cream mixture into the egg yolks. Add the yolk mixture into the pan, whisking as you do.

Add a candy thermometer and return the mixture to the heat until it reaches 85°C or 185°F. If you don't have a thermometer, set a timer for 2 minutes only—note that overheating this mixture will make it curdle. Remove from the heat and immediately pour through the fine sieve onto the chocolate. Leave to sit for 2 minutes. Whisk the chocolate cream mixture until it is combined and smooth.

Remove the pastry shell from the tin and place it on a flat serving plate. Pour the velvety chocolate mixture into the pastry shell until it is brimming. Gently tap the plate on the bench to bring any air bubbles to the surface. Place in the fridge for at least 3 hours to chill and set.

DECORATION

Temper the dark chocolate (see page 48) and pour along one of the long sides of the rectangle of acetate. Using a square notched cake comb, spread the chocolate diagonally across to make lines of chocolate. Lift the acetate and roll it to make a cylinder, then slide into a cup to hold the shape. Leave for 20 minutes for the chocolate to set.

Once the tart is firm, add raspberries to the top, starting at the outside and working your way around the edge, making more circles until you get to the middle. Carefully remove the acetate from the chocolate. Add swirls one at a time, poking one end into the tart.

Video tutorial for this recipe can be found at howtocookthat.net/cookbook

Chocolate Raspberry Tart

BANANA CREAM PIE

This family favorite features crisp pastry lined with milk chocolate, gooey caramel, fresh banana, and whipped cream, all topped off with homemade banana ice cream. Every element of this dessert is yummy on its own, but put it all together, and it's irresistible.

Makes eight 10 cm (4 inch) individual desserts or one 23 cm (9 inch) pie.

PASTRY

¾ cup (185 g / 6.5 oz) chilled butter

2 ¼ cups (360 g / 12.7 oz) plain or all-purpose flour

⅓ cup (70 g / 2.5 oz) caster sugar or superfine sugar

1 egg (45 g / 1.6 oz)

1 tablespoon (15 mL / 0.5 fl oz) milk

DULCE DE LECHE

Makes (400 mL / 13.5 fl oz)

1 quart (1 litre / 0.25 gallons) milk

2 cups (430 g / 15 oz) sugar

3 teaspoons vanilla extract

1 teaspoon baking soda (bi-carb soda)

BANANA ICE CREAM

4 over-ripe bananas (500 g / 17.6 oz)

¼ cup (55 g / 1.9 oz) sugar

¾ cup (200 mL / 6.8 fl oz) milk

6 large egg yolks (90 g / 3.2 oz)

¾ cup (160 g / 5.6 oz) caster sugar or superfine sugar

⅓ cup (100 mL / 3.4 fl oz) heavy cream (35 percent fat)

ASSEMBLY

3.5 oz (100 g) milk chocolate

4 ripe bananas (500 g / 17.6 oz)

1 ¼ cups (300 mL / 10 fl oz) heavy cream (35 percent fat)

PASTRY

Preheat oven to 180°C (350°F).

Using your fingers, rub the butter into the flour until it resembles breadcrumbs. Stir in the sugar, egg, and milk. Squeeze to form a ball of dough. Roll out on baking paper and cut circles of pastry. Use the pastry circles to line either eight 10 cm (4 inch) individual loose-base pie tins, or one 9 inch round pie pan. Using a knife, cut around the top of each tin to neaten it up. Bake in the oven until golden—this will take 20–25 minutes for the small ones or 35–40 minutes for a large one. Remove from the oven and use the bottom of a glass to flatten and push any air out of the base. Leave to cool.

DULCE DE LECHE

Bring the milk to a boil, then add the sugar, vanilla, and baking soda. Stir until the sugar is dissolved.

Reduce the heat and simmer over medium-low heat for 50 minutes, stirring occasionally. Continue to heat for another 10 minutes, stirring continuously. Place a spoonful on a cold plate to check the thickness of the caramel. When it is starting to get really thick on the bottom of the pan, remove it from the heat and strain through a fine sieve into a heatproof bowl. Leave to cool to room temperature.

BANANA ICE CREAM

Follow the directions for strawberry ice cream (on page 158), swapping the strawberries for bananas.

ASSEMBLY

Break the chocolate into pieces and put into a bowl. Microwave for 60 seconds on high and then stir, 30 seconds and then stir, and after that, repeat in 20-second bursts stirring after each until it is completely melted. Pour some of the melted chocolate into each of the 4 individual pastry pans and use a spoon to spread it all around the inside of the pastry. Refrigerate for 10 minutes.

Fill each of the 4 pans three-quarters full with dulce de leche, then add generous slices of fresh banana and pipe or dollop on whipped cream. Just before serving, add a scoop of banana ice cream and drizzle with melted chocolate.

SUGAR SNOW GLOBE DESSERT

There's a hint of Christmas in these eye-catching Snow Globe Desserts with their green pistachio base and bright red raspberries. But really, they are suitable for any time of the year. Each delightful dessert is filled with orange curd, diplomat cream, and fresh fruit, topped with a thin sugar globe.

Makes twelve 7.5 cm (3 inch) mini tarts.

PISTACHIO BASE

½ cup (125 g / 4.4 oz) butter

1 ½ cups (250 g / 8.8 oz) plain or all-purpose flour

¼ cup (35 g / 1.2 oz) pistachios

¼ cup (30 g / 1.1 oz) hazelnuts

½ cups (125 g / 4.4 oz) sugar

1 egg (45 g / 1.6 oz)

1 drop green gel food coloring

12 x 3 inch (7.5 cm) loose-based baking pans or a muffin tin.

ORANGE CURD

2 cups (500 mL / 16.9 fl oz) fresh orange juice

¾ tablespoon powdered gelatin

Zest of one orange

½ cup (125 g / 4.4 oz) sugar

3 eggs (135 g / 4.8 oz)

1 cup (200 g / 7 oz) butter, cubed

DIPLOMAT CREAM

1 tablespoon (8 g / 0.3 oz) corn flour or cornstarch

3 tablespoons (40 g / 1.4 oz) sugar

1 egg yolk (15 g / 0.5 oz)

¼ cup (60 mL / 2 fl oz) heavy cream (35 percent fat)

¼ cup (60 mL / 2 fl oz) milk

An additional ½ cup (125 mL / 4.2 fl oz) heavy cream (35 percent fat)

Piping bag

Star-shaped piping tip

SUGAR DOME

1 ⅓ cups (300 g / 10.6 oz) sugar

⅓ cup (75 mL / 2.5 fl oz) water

½ cup (200 g / 7 oz) glucose syrup or light corn syrup

Silicone hemisphere mold, each cavity ⅓ cup (80 mL / 2.7 fl oz)

Pastry brush

PISTACHIO BASE

Rub the butter into the flour until it resembles fine breadcrumbs. Put the pistachios and hazelnuts into a Ziploc bag and crush them into fine pieces by hitting them with a rolling pin. Alternatively, you could use a food processor for this step. Add the nuts to the flour mixture along with the sugar and stir well. Beat together the egg and green food coloring. Add this into the flour mixture and stir well until it forms a ball. Wrap in plastic wrap and refrigerate for 30 minutes.

Preheat the oven to 180°C (350°F). Line the base of your muffin tin cups or loose-based pans with a circle of baking paper in each one. Roll out the pastry on a piece of plastic wrap. Cut a 2 cm strip of pastry using a pizza cutter, pushing down firmly enough to cut through the plastic wrap as well. Pick up the strip with the wrap and put the pastry side around the inside of your cups or tins so it is touching the base. Trim to size and remove the plastic. Cut circles of pastry and add to the center of each tin or muffin cup, using your fingers to make sure each circle is joined to the edges.

Place onto a baking sheet and bake in the oven for 10 minutes. Set aside to cool.

ORANGE CURD

Add 3 tablespoons of the orange juice to the gelatin; stir it through immediately, then leave it to absorb the liquid.

Place the orange zest, remaining orange juice, and sugar in a pan. Bring to a boil and reduce heat, continuing to simmer until it concentrates down to 1 cup (250 mL / 8.4 fl oz). Add in the gelatin and stir until melted.

Beat the eggs and pour into the juice and sugar mixture, whisking as you do. Stir continuously for a few minutes over high heat until it thickens. Remove from the stove, add the butter, and stir until it is melted. Strain the mixture through a sieve to get rid of the orange zest. Leave to cool.

DIPLOMAT CREAM

In a bowl, whisk together the corn flour, sugar and egg yolk. Add 2 tablespoons of the cream and whisk again to make a smooth paste.

Heat the milk and 2 fl oz (60 mL) of cream in a saucepan until it just starts to boil, then slowly add it to the egg yolk mixture, whisking as you do. Return the mixture to the pan and stir over the heat until it thickens. Continue to stir over high heat for another 60 seconds. Pour it into a flat dish and cover with plastic wrap to stop it forming a skin. Place in the fridge for 2 hours to cool.

Candy thermometer

Circle cookie cutter

ASSEMBLY

24 (100 g / 3.5 oz) raspberries

36 (20 g / 0.7 oz) blueberries

12 (150 g / 5.3 oz) strawberries

Once it is chilled, whip the additional cream to form soft peaks. Take three large spoons of whipped cream and whisk it into the custard to lighten it, then fold in the rest of the whipped cream. Place into a piping bag with a star-shaped tip.

SUGAR DOME

Spray the underside of the silicone hemisphere mold with a little cooking oil and rub it over the surface so the sugar doesn't stick.

Place the sugar, water, and glucose syrup in a pan over high heat. Once it starts to boil, wash down the sides of the pan using a wet pastry brush.

Heat to 150°C (302°F), then immediately remove from the stovetop and cool to 130°C (266°F).

Place the silicone mold on a chopping board, propped up at an angle so any excess sugar syrup can run down. Add some baking paper underneath to protect the counter.

Pour the hot sugar syrup in a circular motion over each mold so they are completely covered.

As the sugar starts to cool, push firmly down around the base of each hemisphere with a greased circle cookie cutter.

Once it is completely cold, you can peel away the silicone mold. Press up in the center of each hemisphere to remove it from the surrounding sugar. Store in an airtight container at room temperature until you are ready to use.

ASSEMBLY

Wash and dry the berries. Cut the strawberries in half vertically. Remove the pistachio pastry shells from their tins. Place heaped tablespoons of orange curd into each tart shell. Pipe little stars of diplomat cream all over the top of the orange curd.

Add 3 blueberries, 2 raspberries, and half a strawberry to each dessert. Store in the fridge until you're ready to serve; then finally, add a sugar dome and present your creation to the table.

Video tutorial for this recipe can be found at howtocookthat.net/cookbook

Sugar Snow Globe Dessert

ROSE APPLE PIE

A delicious bouquet of gorgeous red apple roses with rich creamy custard in a crisp pecan pastry. It's beautiful enough to take center stage on a dessert buffet...but why wait for a big occasion when you could share it over afternoon tea with old friends?

When apples are heated, the flesh softens and the red skins turns a dull reddish brown. In this recipe, you will learn my secret to softening apples as if they are cooked without losing the bright red color of the skin.

Makes one 10 inch rose apple pie, yielding 8-10 servings.

PECAN PASTRY

½ cup (125 g / 4.4 oz) unsalted butter

1 ½ cups (250 g / 8.8 oz) plain or all-purpose flour

½ cup (100 g / 3.5 oz) caster sugar or superfine sugar

½ cup (60 g / 2.1 oz) pecan nuts, processed until fine

1 egg (45 g / 1.6 oz)

JAM GLAZE

¼ cup (80 g / 2.8 oz) strawberry jam

1 tablespoon water

CUSTARD

4 egg yolks (60 g / 2.1 oz)

3 tablespoons (37 g / 1.3 oz) caster sugar or superfine sugar

2 tablespoons (14 g / 0.5 oz) cornstarch

¾ cup (200 mL / 6.8 fl oz) milk

½ cup (100 mL / 3.4 fl oz) heavy cream (35 percent fat)

2 teaspoons vanilla extract

RED APPLE ROSES

½ cup (105 g / 3.7 oz) sugar

½ cup (110 g / 3.9 oz) melted butter

½ cup (125 mL / 4.2 fl oz) fresh orange juice

28 medium or 18 large red apples— look for large apples that are red all over

PECAN PASTRY

Preheat the oven to 180°C (350°F). Rub the butter into the flour until it resembles fine breadcrumbs. Stir in the pecans and sugar. Add the egg and stir through, then squeeze it together to form a ball of pastry dough.

Roll your pastry out thinly between two sheets of plastic wrap until it is a little bigger than the pie dish. Peel off the top layer of plastic. Using the plastic wrap that is underneath the pastry, flip the pastry over onto the 25 cm (10 inch) pie dish. Use the plastic to help you position it so the pastry is lining the dish, then peel off the plastic wrap. Trim around the top edge. Using a fork, press small holes across the base to get rid of any air bubbles—this ensures it will cook flat and evenly. Bake your base in the oven for 30-40 minutes or until it is crisp and golden.

JAM GLAZE

Heat the jam and water in a saucepan until it is bubbling hot, then strain through a fine sieve into a heatproof bowl. Brush the hot jam all over the inside of the cooked pastry shell.

CUSTARD

In a pan, whisk together the yolks, sugar, and cornstarch, making sure there are no lumps. Add a little of the milk at a time, whisking it in. Place over high heat and stir continuously until it thickens. Continue stirring for another 60 seconds. Remove from the heat and whisk in the cream and vanilla. Pour the warm custard into the base and spread it out.

RED APPLE ROSES

Combine the sugar, melted butter, and orange juice in a bowl.

Working with two apples at a time, slice them finely with a mandolin to make circles of apple. Place the slices into the orange juice mixture and leave to soak for ten minutes.

Your apples will now be softened like they have been cooked but will retain the redness of their skin. Take a circle of apple and roll it into a tube shape. Wrap another piece of apple around it as if you were adding petals and continue to do this until you're happy with the appearance of your "rose." Trim a very small amount off one end of the cylinder of apple to flatten it, and push the rose into the custard near the edge of the tart. Rest a knife across the pie dish to hold the rose in place while you make the next one. Continue to make more apple roses and add them until the custard is covered and the pie is full.

This step is easy, but it is time-consuming, so invite over a friend to help and have a long chat and a laugh while you do it. Then refrigerate until you are ready to serve.

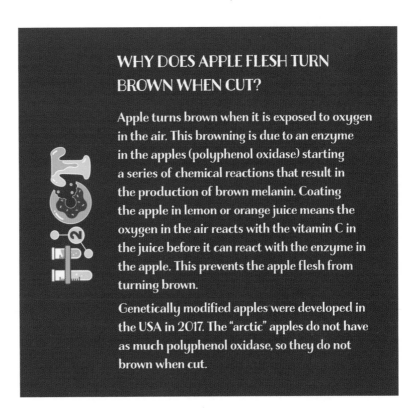

WHY DOES APPLE FLESH TURN BROWN WHEN CUT?

Apple turns brown when it is exposed to oxygen in the air. This browning is due to an enzyme in the apples (polyphenol oxidase) starting a series of chemical reactions that result in the production of brown melanin. Coating the apple in lemon or orange juice means the oxygen in the air reacts with the vitamin C in the juice before it can react with the enzyme in the apple. This prevents the apple flesh from turning brown.

Genetically modified apples were developed in the USA in 2017. The "arctic" apples do not have as much polyphenol oxidase, so they do not brown when cut.

Video tutorial for this recipe can be found at howtocookthat.net/cookbook

Rose Apple Pie

MACARON CHOCOLATE TART

This delightful dessert might be too much for some home bakers, but you can always try just one of the elements. The mousse is lovely served in small glasses and macarons are a perennial favorite.

Makes one 8 inch (20 cm) tart.

ORANGE CRÈME BRÛLÉE

1 cup (250 mL / 8.4 fl oz) heavy cream (35 percent fat)

3 tablespoons (36 g / 1.3 oz) sugar

Zest of one orange, grated

2 egg yolks (35 g / 1.2 oz)

PASTRY SHELL

½ cup (125 g / 4.4 oz) butter

1 ¼ cups (200 g / 7 oz) plain or all-purpose flour

¼ cup (50 g / 1.8 oz) sugar

1 egg (45 g / 1.6 oz)

½ teaspoon vanilla extract

Ceramic baking weights or you can use uncooked rice or dried beans

8-inch (20 cm) loose-based baking pan (a springform pan or one with a removable base)

3.5 oz (100 g) milk chocolate

RASPBERRY GLAZE

¼ cup (75 mL / 2.5 fl oz) raspberry puree

1 teaspoon (5 g / 0.2 oz) powdered gelatin

2 tablespoons (13 g / 0.5 oz) corn flour or cornstarch

2 teaspoons (15 g / 0.5 oz) glucose syrup or light corn syrup

2 tablespoons (30 mL / 1 fl oz) water

⅔ cup (140 g / 5 oz) sugar

¾ cup (175 g / 6.1 oz) heavy cream (35 percent fat)

Red food coloring

4 oz (115 g) white chocolate

CHOCOLATE MOUSSE

½ teaspoon (2 g / 0.1 oz) powdered gelatin

⅔ cup (165 mL / 5.6 fl oz) heavy cream (35 percent fat)

4 tablespoons (60 mL / 2 fl oz) milk

1 teaspoon (5 g / 0.2 oz) sugar

ORANGE CRÈME BRÛLÉE

Preheat the oven to 150°C (300°F).

Heat the cream, sugar, and orange zest in a saucepan until it starts to boil. Remove from the heat and let sit for 15 minutes to infuse the orange flavor.

Whisk the egg yolks in a bowl. Then whisk in the warm cream and strain the mixture through a sieve into a 5 inch (13 cm) dome-shaped bowl. Put the bowl into a deep baking dish partially filled with water. The water level should nearly match the cream level inside of the bowl. This water bath stops the brûlée overheating and splitting into a lumpy mess.

Bake in the oven for approximately 25 minutes. When ready, it should be set but still a little wobbly in the center. Remove from the oven and allow to cool for an hour, then cover with plastic wrap and place in the freezer.

PASTRY SHELL

Preheat the oven to 180°C (350°F).

Grease a loose-based pastry pan (a springform pan or one with a removable base). Separate the base from the side of the tin or pan and put a circle of nonstick baking paper on the base.

Rub the butter and flour together using your fingers until they look like breadcrumbs. Add the sugar, egg, and vanilla. Stir until combined, then use your hands to squeeze the mixture into a ball.

Roll the pastry out between two sheets of plastic wrap. Peel off the top layer of plastic; then, using the plastic underneath as a support, flip the pastry over onto the base of the pan. Remove the rest of the plastic. Use a knife to trim around the edge and put the base back into the pan. Shape the remaining pastry into a thick snake and roll out between two sheets of plastic wrap to make a long rectangle. Use a pizza cutter to cut two 1 inch (2.5 cm) strips. Remove the top layer of plastic and position the strip of pastry around the side of the pan so it is joining to the base. Remove the remaining plastic and repeat for the second strip so that you have pastry all the way around the edge of the tart.

Line with nonstick baking paper and add ceramic baking weights on top of the paper. Bake for 10 minutes, then remove the weights and the paper and return to the oven for a further 10–15 minutes or until golden.

Put the chocolate into a bowl and microwave for 60 seconds on high, stir, then microwave 30 seconds and stir. Keep doing 30-second bursts and stirring until there are no lumps left. Pour into the pastry pan and spread all over the base and sides. This keeps the pastry crisp by creating a barrier between it and the mousse.

1 egg yolk (15 g / 0.5 oz)

1.8 oz (50 g) milk chocolate

1.8 oz (50 g) dark chocolate

PASSIONFRUIT GANACHE

10.6 oz (300 g) milk chocolate

⅓ cup (100 mL / 3.4 fl oz) passionfruit syrup without seeds

MACARONS

1 ¾ cup (220 g / 7.8 oz) icing sugar or powdered sugar

1 cup (120 g / 4.2 oz) almond flour

4 egg whites (120 g / 4.2 oz)

⅓ cup (80 g / 2.8 oz) caster sugar or superfine sugar

1 teaspoon yellow powdered food color

RASPBERRY GLAZE

Add 2 tablespoons of raspberry puree to the gelatin and mix quickly together. In a separate bowl, add 2 tablespoons of raspberry puree to the corn flour and mix well.

Heat the glucose syrup, water, and sugar over high heat until the sugar is dissolved. Mix in the cream, raspberry puree, and the corn flour mixture. Bring back up to the boil, stirring continuously. Stir for 1 minute as it boils and thickens. Take off the heat, add gelatin mixture, and stir until melted. Add one drop of red food coloring at a time until your desired color is reached. Break the white chocolate into pieces and place into a bowl. Strain raspberry mixture through a sieve onto the white chocolate, wait two minutes, then whisk together. Set aside to cool to room temperature.

CHOCOLATE MOUSSE

Place the gelatin in a small bowl and add a tablespoon of the milk, then mix immediately and set aside.

Whip the cream to form soft peaks.

Combine the milk, sugar, and egg yolks in a pan. Stir continuously and heat to 86°C (186.8°F). Remove from the heat and stir through the gelatin until it is melted. Strain through a sieve onto the chocolate, wait a couple of minutes, then whisk well to combine.

Cool to room temperature, but don't put it in the fridge or it will set. Fold in the cream using a spatula and pour into the chocolate-lined pastry shell. Place in the fridge to set.

PASSIONFRUIT GANACHE

Heat passionfruit syrup in the microwave, then pour over your chocolate. Wait two minutes before stirring with a whisk to combine. Leave to cool to room temperature.

MACARONS

Preheat the oven to 150°C (300°F). Using a coarse sieve, sift the icing sugar and almond flour together. Discard any gritty bits of almond flour left behind (there should not be more than a teaspoonful).

Beat the egg whites and sugar together on high speed until stiff. Whisk for an additional 2 minutes to dry the egg whites, then add the color. NOTE: Liquid color can ruin macarons, so use oil-based or powdered food color.

Add the almond sugar mixture and fold in using a rubber spatula. Once you can no longer see any almond flour, keep gently folding until the mixture looks like lava.

If you drop some mixture off the spatula into the bowl, it should droop down very slowly—it shouldn't be runny. While you are folding, periodically scrape down the sides of the bowl and the spatula to make sure everything is mixed in uniformly.

Place a sheet of nonstick baking paper over the template (page 181). Spoon the mixture into a piping bag and pipe small circles. Slide the paper onto a baking sheet, then bang the baking sheet on the bench firmly several times. This gets rid of air bubbles and helps prevent cracking.

Place into the oven (you do not need to leave them to sit on the bench with this recipe) and bake until a foot has formed and the shells are crisp. This takes approximately 20 minutes. Try not to open the oven unnecessarily during the cooking process as this can cause a drop in temperature and make your macarons hollow. To check if they are done, open the oven and gently press down on the top of a macaron. If it squashes down at the foot it is not ready, so quickly close the oven and give them a few more minutes.

Once they are ready, remove from the oven, cool, and then gently peel off the baking paper. Hold the shells together to "match" pairs that are the most similar in size. Sandwich together in pairs using passionfruit ganache. Place them flat in an airtight container in the fridge until needed.

ASSEMBLY

Take the brûlée out of the freezer and place the bowl into a larger container of hot water to loosen it. Dry the bowl and tip the brûlée out, then balance it on a drinking glass that is sitting on a large plate.

If the glaze is set, warm it in the microwave for 20 seconds to soften. However, you do not want the glaze to be hot. Ladle the glaze over the brûlée, letting the excess drip down. For a more intense color, you can return the brûlée to the freezer for 10 minutes, then add another layer of glaze. Using a knife, remove any drips of glaze hanging down from the base. Carefully lift up the brûlée using an offset spatula and add it to the center of the chocolate mousse.

And for your final touch, add your macarons around the outside of the brûlée.

Video tutorial for this recipe can be found at howtocookthat.net/cookbook

SWEET CHERRY PIE

I love fresh cherries! As a university student, I had a casual job in an extremely busy department store. My favorite part of the day was walking across the mall to a fruit and veg shop to buy a small bag of cherries on my lunch break. Many years later, this Sweet Cherry Pie recipe has become one of my favorites. I actually can't bear the thought of cooking this beautiful fruit, so this dessert has fresh cherries as the hero ingredient.

Makes 1 tart, 14 x 5 inch (35 x 13 cm).

PASTRY

Zest of one lime or lemon

½ cup (120 g / 4.2 oz) butter

¾ cup (95 g / 3.3 oz) icing sugar or powdered sugar

1 egg (45 g / 1.6 oz)

⅓ cup (35 g / 1.2 oz) almond meal or almond flour

1 ½ cups (240 g / 8.5 oz) plain or all-purpose flour

Ceramic baking weights or you can use uncooked rice or dried beans

FILLING

1 cup (225 g / 8 oz) block cream cheese

3 tablespoons (35 g / 1.2 oz) caster sugar or superfine sugar

1 teaspoon vanilla extract

1 cup (240 mL / 8 fl oz) heavy cream (35 percent fat)

TOPPING

3 pounds (1.3 kg) fresh cherries

¼ cup (80 g / 2.8 oz) seedless raspberry jam

PASTRY

Preheat your oven to 180°C (350°F).

Using an electric mixer, whisk together the zest, butter, and powdered sugar until creamy. Add the egg and whisk some more. Mix in the almond meal and then finally the flour. Keep mixing until it just starts to clump together. Press together with your hands to form a ball, then place it between two sheets of plastic wrap. Using a rolling pin, roll it out to be slightly bigger than the size of your tin. Remove the top layer of plastic. Using the plastic underneath to support the pastry, lift it up and flip it over onto the tin. Gently press into all the corners, then remove the top layer of plastic. Use a knife to trim off the excess pastry from around the edge. Line with baking paper and add ceramic baking weights on top of the paper. Bake in the oven for 10-15 minutes. Remove the paper and baking weights, then bake for a further 3-5 minutes or until golden. Cool in the tin.

FILLING

Using an electric mixer, whip together the cream cheese and sugar until the mixture is smooth and creamy. Add the vanilla and half of the cream. Whisk well. Add the remaining cream and whisk until thick and fluffy.

Remove the pastry shell from the tin and put onto a serving platter. Put the filling in the center and use a spatula to spread it out evenly.

TOPPING

Wash and pit the cherries. Add a layer of cherries neatly in rows to cover the filling. Then stack a second layer of cherries on top. Heat the jam in the microwave until it is runny. Use a pastry brush to brush a layer of hot jam over the cherries.

Video tutorial for this recipe can be found at howtocookthat.net/cookbook

THE CROQUEMBOUCHE

Croquembouche (pronounced crockenbush) are beautiful towers of pastry cream-filled profiteroles held together with caramelized sugar. It is a truly impressive centerpiece, yet surprisingly easy to make. If you want an easier option, you can of course make individual profiteroles and top each one with melted milk chocolate.

This recipe makes one croquembouche 11 inches (27 cm) tall and 4 inches (10 cm) in diameter at the base. Serves 15 people.

CHOUX PASTRY
1 cup (250 mL / 8.4 fl oz) water
⅓ cup (75 g / 2.6 oz) butter
1 cup (160 g / 5.6 oz) plain or
    all-purpose flour
4 eggs (180 g / 6.3 oz)

PASTRY CREAM
4 egg yolks (60 g / 2.1 oz)
¾ cup (164 g / 5.8 oz) sugar
3 tablespoons (30 g / 1.1 oz) plain or
    all-purpose flour
1 teaspoon vanilla extract
2 cups (500 mL / 16.9 fl oz) milk

CRISPY CARAMEL & ANGEL HAIR
½ cup (150 mL / 5 fl oz) water
2 cups (450 g / 15.9 oz) sugar
1 tablespoon (21 g / 0.7 oz) glucose
    syrup or light corn syrup

ASSEMBLY
Violas a.k.a. violets (or other small
    edible flowers)

CHOUX PASTRY
Heat the oven to 425°F (220°C).

Place the water and butter in a saucepan and heat until melted. Add the flour all at once and stir until the mixture thickens and leaves the sides of the pan. Continue to stir over heat for another 60 seconds until it forms a really stiff ball. Remove from the heat and add the eggs one at a time, mixing well after each addition using electric beaters.

Place into a piping bag and pipe small dollops about the size of a strawberry onto the baking sheet. Allow a little room for spreading, as choux pastry puffs up in the oven.

Bake for 20 minutes or until golden and crisp.

PASTRY CREAM
Whip together the egg yolks, sugar, flour, and vanilla. Place the milk in a pan and heat until it just begins to boil. While whisking, add a little of the hot milk into the egg yolk mixture. Whisk in the remaining hot milk and return the mixture to the pan. Stir over high heat until thickened. Place in a heatproof bowl and cover with plastic wrap, then push the wrap down so it is touching the surface of the pastry cream. Allow to cool to room temperature.

CRISPY CARAMEL AND ANGEL HAIR
Make this element after your croquembouche is assembled as it needs to be used immediately. Place the sugar, water, and glucose syrup into a pan over high heat, stirring until the sugar is dissolved. Wash down the sides of the pan with a wet pastry brush. Leave bubbling over high heat unstirred for about 6 minutes or until it just starts to go golden. Watch carefully from 4 minutes onwards as it can turn from golden to burnt very quickly. Remove from the heat. Carefully pour a spoonful of your caramel into a glass of cold water and check that it sets solid. If it is still soft or can be squashed, then put the pan back over the heat for one more minute and repeat the test. (Be extra careful with this step as the caramel is hotter than boiling water.)

ASSEMBLY
Place the pastry cream into a piping bag or a Ziploc bag with the corner cut off. Make a small hole in the side of each profiterole and pipe in the pastry cream until you feel the profiterole just start to bulge.

Make a cone out of cardboard that is 27 cm (11 inches) tall and 10 cm (4 inches) in diameter at the base. Secure it using staples and sticky tape. Check that it stands up straight, then line the inside of the cone with nonstick baking paper.

The caramel will absorb moisture from the air and soften, so the following step should be done within 1 hour of serving.

Secure your cardboard cone upside down. Wear two silicone gloves on each hand to protect you from the heat of the caramel. Dip one half of a profiterole into the hot caramel, then place it inside the pointy end of the cone. Continue to place caramel dipped profiteroles all the way around the inside edge of the cone until you get to the top. Allow it to cool for 10 minutes. Place a plate on top and flip over so that the cone is now sitting upright. Remove the cardboard and then the baking paper, leaving you a cone of profiteroles.

Place some baking paper over a deep container so the paper goes up over each side and down in the middle. Cut the loops off a wire whisk so you have prongs, or alternatively use two forks. Dip the prongs into the slightly cooled caramel and run your tool back and forth across the container to make fine strands of caramel or "Angel Hair." If your caramel has set too firm, you can either reheat it on the stovetop or make a fresh batch. Once you have a good amount of finely pulled sugar, wrap it around the croquembouche. Repeat to make more, then wrap it around the top. Add the edible flowers. Serve your croquembouche immediately.

Video tutorial for this recipe can be found at howtocookthat.net/cookbook

BAKED CHURROS WITH CHOCOLATE SAUCE

Churros are a guaranteed hit with my hungry boys. A stack of hot, cinnamon sugar churros accompanied by little pots of melted chocolate are always perfect for a party or special dinner. In this recipe, I will show you how to make both traditional fried churros and my own baked version, which is slightly healthier and much quicker to make at home in large quantities.

Makes seventeen 9 inch (23 cm) churros, which should be plenty for 5 people.

CHURROS

1 cup (250 mL / 8.4 fl oz) water
½ cup (110 g / 3.9 oz) butter
1 cup (160 g / 5.6 oz) plain or
   all-purpose flour
3 eggs (135 g / 4.8 oz)
1 tablespoon (15 g / 0.5 oz) sugar
1 teaspoon vanilla
Strong pastry piping bag
Large star-shaped piping nozzle
1 quart (1 litre) vegetable oil for
   frying (optional)

CINNAMON SUGAR

4 tablespoons (30 g / 1 oz) sugar
1 teaspoon ground cinnamon

CHOCOLATE POTS

3.5 oz (100 g) milk chocolate
3.5 oz (100 g) white chocolate

CHURROS

Place the water and butter in a pan and heat until the butter is melted. Add the flour, stirring continuously. Keep stirring over the heat until the mixture thickens, clumps together, and starts to form a ball.

Remove from the heat; using a spoon, briskly stir in the eggs one at a time.

Add the vanilla and sugar and combine. Spoon your mixture into a piping bag fitted with a star-shaped nozzle.

For fried curly churros, heat the oil in a pan to 182°C (360°F). Pipe the churro batter straight into the hot oil. Use a knife to break off the batter when it is the required length. Fry until browned, then lift out and drain on a plate covered in several layers of paper towels.

For straight baked churros, preheat the oven to 180°C (350°F). Pipe long snakes of churro batter onto a baking sheet lined with nonstick baking paper. (Note that if you want to make these ahead of time, you can freeze the piped churros and store for up to a month.) Spray the churros lightly with cooking oil. Bake in the oven for 17–20 minutes or until crisp on the outside and soft in the middle.

As soon as your churros come out of the hot oil or oven, sprinkle with cinnamon sugar and serve hot with chocolate pots.

CHOCOLATE POTS

Melt the milk chocolate in the microwave for 60 seconds on high and stir, microwave 30 seconds and stir, then repeat in 20-second bursts, stirring each time until it is melted. Pour the chocolate into a small serving bowl. Follow the same procedure for the white chocolate. Serve immediately with hot churros.

Video tutorial for this recipe can be found at howtocookthat.net/cookbook

ITALIAN CANNOLI

One of my favorite treats, apart from gelato, is crispy cannoli. So when planning a trip to Italy, I was excited to book a private lesson for my son and I to learn how to make these sweet treats the traditional way. Our charming Sicilian chef was happy for us to film and share the recipe with you.

Makes 25 cannoli tubes.

CANNOLI TUBES

1 ¾ cups (250 g / 8.8 oz) plain or
  all-purpose flour

1 egg (45 g / 1.6 oz)

1 teaspoon cinnamon

¼ cup sugar (50 g / 1.8 oz)

¼ cup (50 g / 1.8 oz) butter, slightly
  melted

2–4 tablespoons (30–60 mL /
  1–2 fl oz) Marsala or red wine

⅓ cup (50 g / 1.8 oz) semolina flour
  for rolling

3 inch (8 cm) round cookie cutter

Metal cannoli tubes

Metal skimmer spoon (or other
  all-metal sieve)

½ gallon (2 litres) oil for deep-frying

RICOTTA FILLING
(Enough to fill 25 cannoli)

1 ¾ cups (500 g / 17.6 oz) ricotta

1 cup (200 g / 7 oz) sugar

⅓ cup (45 g / 1.6 oz) candied dried
  fruits

CREMA BIANCA FILLING
(Enough to fill 25 cannoli)

5 egg yolks (75 g / 2.6 oz)

½ cup milk (125 mL / 4 fl oz)

⅔ cup (140 g / 4.9 oz) sugar

Zest of ½ a lime

Zest of 1 orange

2 tablespoons (30 mL / 1 fl oz) orange
  juice

⅓ cup (50 g / 1.8 oz) semolina flour

2 cups (500 mL / 16 fl oz) milk

ASSEMBLY

⅓ cup (50 g / 1.8 oz) chopped almonds

⅓ cup (50 g / 1.8 oz) chopped
  pistachios

1.8 oz (50 g) small chocolate chips or
  chopped chocolate

CANNOLI TUBES

Tip the flour onto the counter in a small pile and make a hole in the center. Add the egg into the hole and use your hands to combine. Once it is mixed in, it will still be dry and crumbly. Tip the cinnamon and sugar on top and mix through. Pour on the slightly melted butter and mix it in, still using your hands. Add the Marsala a little at a time until you get a firm dough. Knead for a few minutes until it is smooth. Wrap it in plastic wrap and rest in the fridge overnight.

Dust the surface with semolina flour. Roll out the dough to about ¹⁄₁₆ inch (2 mm) thick. Cut circles using the cookie cutter. Now roll each circle out so that it is larger and thinner. Each one should be thin enough that you can see the silhouette of your fingers through the dough when you hold it toward the light.

Wrap the circle of dough around the cannoli tube. They should be big enough to wrap all the way around the tube and overlap by about 1.5 cm (½ inch). Use your finger to put a little egg on the dough where it overlaps to ensure it sticks together.

Heat your oil to 188°C (370°F).

If you are using metal cannoli tubes, they will sink to the bottom of your oil. To prevent this from happening, place three at a time onto a skimmer (or all-metal sieve) and lower into the hot oil. The cannoli shells should puff up with bubbles all over them, this is a sign of a good cannoli. Once they are golden, lift them out, but be careful to tilt them over the pan to allow the oil to drain out of the tubes. Place your tubes onto a paper towel and let them cool.

Squeeze the metal tube to make it smaller and slide it out of the cannoli shell. Look at the inside to check that it is cooked all the way through. If not, you can always return your shells to the pan and fry them for a little longer.

Do not reroll the spare dough that was between the circles because the semolina flour is only supposed to be on the outside. You can, however, fry up the scraps and drizzle with warm Nutella as a bonus treat.

RICOTTA FILLING

Whisk together the ricotta and sugar. Add in the candied fruits and mix through. Store covered in the fridge until you are ready to use it. You can use chopped chocolate in your filling instead of candied fruit if you prefer.

CREMA BIANCA FILLING

Whisk together the egg yolks, ½ cup milk, sugar, lime zest, orange zest, orange juice, and semolina flour in a bowl until there are no lumps. Heat 2 cups of milk in a saucepan until it just starts to boil.

Pour in the egg yolk mixture, whisking as you do. Stir continuously over the heat until it starts to bubble and thicken. Keep stirring over the heat for another 60 seconds. Tip into a bowl, cover in plastic wrap, and allow it to cool in the fridge for at least two hours.

ASSEMBLY

Place the filling into a piping bag or a Ziploc bag with the corner cut off. Pipe your filling into each tube. Dip each end into chopped pistachios, almonds, or chocolate. Eat within 3 hours of filling or the shells will go soggy. Unfilled shells can be stored in an airtight container for a few days.

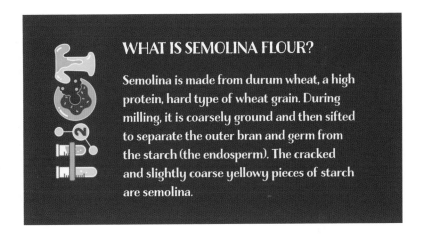

WHAT IS SEMOLINA FLOUR?

Semolina is made from durum wheat, a high protein, hard type of wheat grain. During milling, it is coarsely ground and then sifted to separate the outer bran and germ from the starch (the endosperm). The cracked and slightly coarse yellowy pieces of starch are semolina.

Video tutorial for this recipe can be found at howtocookthat.net/cookbook

Italian Cannoli

COFFEE DONUT MILLEFEUILLE

I've never been a coffee lover. I don't drink it at home, and when I go to a café, I prefer hot chocolate. And yet, I love coffee-flavored desserts...which is why I developed this recipe celebrating the famous duo of coffee and donuts.

Makes 6.

PASTRY

3 square sheets puff pastry

2 tablespoons icing sugar or powdered sugar

DONUT CREAM

1 cinnamon donut

¾ cup (200 mL / 6.8 fl oz) heavy cream (35 percent fat)

1 teaspoon vanilla

1 tablespoon (8 g / 0.3 oz) icing sugar or powdered sugar

½ teaspoon cinnamon

Additional ½ cup (100 mL / 3.4 fl oz) heavy cream (35 percent fat)

COFFEE CREAM

1 teaspoon instant coffee granules

1 tablespoon boiling water

1 cup (260 mL / 8.5 fl oz) heavy cream (35 percent fat)

2.8 oz (80 g) white chocolate

ASSEMBLY

2 tablespoons raspberry jam

2 cups (270 g / 9.5 oz) fresh raspberries

1 tablespoon icing sugar or powdered sugar

PASTRY

Preheat the oven to 180°C (350°F).

Cut each sheet of pastry into eight rectangles measuring 2½ x 5 inches (6 x 12 cm). Place onto a flat baking sheet (with no sides) covered with baking paper. Sprinkle icing sugar through a sieve over the top.

Put an empty baking sheet into the oven to heat. At the same time, bake the pastry for ten minutes or until puffed and golden. Remove from the oven and place baking paper over the pastry. Put the hot empty baking sheet on top and press down using an oven glove to flatten the pastry. Return to the oven with the baking sheet still on top for 10-13 minutes or until the sugar is starting to melt. Watch carefully so they don't burn. Rotate them from the outside into the middle if necessary.

TIP: If you don't have a flat baking sheet that has no sides, turn a normal baking pan upside down.

DONUT CREAM

Break the donut into small chunks and place into a pan with ¾ cup heavy cream and the vanilla, icing sugar, and cinnamon. Stir over high heat. Once it begins to boil, whisk until the donut breaks down and the mixture is a smooth paste. Remove from the heat and whisk through the additional ½ cup cream. Place the bowl in the freezer to cool for 1 hour.

Whisk with electric beaters until you get stiff peaks, then place into a piping bag fitted with a large round nozzle.

COFFEE CREAM

Dissolve the coffee in boiling water. Place the cream, white chocolate, and coffee into a bowl and microwave for 60 seconds on high, stir, then microwave for another minute. Leave to sit for a few minutes, then whisk until smooth.

Place the bowl in the freezer for 1 hour. Using an electric mixer, whisk until you have stiff peaks. Place into a piping bag fitted with a large round nozzle.

ASSEMBLY

Pipe a thin stripe of raspberry jam down the center of twelve pastry rectangles. Pipe dollops of coffee cream along each side on six rectangles. Do the same with your donut cream on another six rectangles. Break three raspberries into pieces and put some on top of each jam stripe. Stack the donut cream rectangles on top of the coffee cream ones. Put a plain rectangle on top and add more fresh raspberries. Sprinkle lightly with icing sugar.

WE ALL
SCREAM
FOR ICE
CREAM

WE ALL SCREAM FOR ICE CREAM

My first date with Dave was on a warm Saturday night in Fremantle, an ocean side town in Western Australia famous for its little Italian cafes along the so-called "Cappuccino Strip." Over our years as a young couple, and then later on as parents with boisterous boys, we would inevitably end up in "Freo" most weekends, grabbing a bite to eat or splashing around on a nearby beach. For such a small town, there seemed to be an abundance of ice cream and gelato shops (my favorite!). As a kid, I'd always loved store-bought ice cream, but nothing could compare with the creamy, flavor-filled goodness to be found down in Freo.

To successfully reproduce such a beautiful treat at home requires some understanding of the basic science behind ice cream. While getting the flavor perfect is actually relatively simple, there is a real art to getting the texture right.

If we simplify the components in ice cream, it is basically made from water (milk is 80 percent water), sugar, fat (cream is 35 percent fat, and egg yolks are 30 percent fat), other solids (like the protein in milk), and air.

WATER AND CHURNING METHODS

When you freeze water, it forms large ice crystals, which line up with each other neatly like tiny bricks on a wall, setting into a solid block of ice. Similarly, if you place your ice cream mixture in a container and into the freezer, it will set into a hard block that can only be chipped away at by using your spoon as jackhammer.

Generally speaking, the larger the ice crystals, the harder and grittier the ice cream will be, so a major goal when making ice cream is to keep those ice crystals as small as possible. This is done in several ways: one of them is churning the ice cream as it freezes, and another is freezing it as fast as possible. To achieve this, ice creameries use commercial ice cream machines that generally cost tens of thousands of dollars.

For at-home bakers, many stand mixers have an ice cream bowl attachment that is a great alternative. It's important that you leave the ice cream bowl in the freezer for at least 24 hours before use. If you freeze the bowl for just a few hours, it will simply not be cold enough to rapidly cool the ice cream mixture and you will end up with bigger ice crystals. For this same reason, you want to make sure you allow your ice cream mixture to chill completely before adding it into the bowl. A warm mixture will take longer to freeze, resulting in bigger ice crystals.

As an alternative, you can use a normal stand mixer with a paddle attachment and crushed dry ice. Dry ice is -80°C or -112°F, so it's perfectly suited to rapidly freezing liquids. A word of caution, though: dry ice is so cold that it can burn your skin, so use gloves or tongs. Place the dry ice into a clean folded cloth, and either bash with a rolling pin or break it up in a food processor or blender to get a fine powder. With the mixer running on low speed, add spoonfuls of dry ice into the ice cream mixture. NOTE: This creates an impressive sinking cloud of cold, white, nontoxic carbon dioxide, so it can be fun to do in front of your guests. It will only take about 3 minutes to freeze. Allow it to churn for 2 more minutes just to make sure there is no dry ice left in the ice cream. Serve immediately.

Another option used by some cafes is -196°C (-320°F) liquid nitrogen. When poured into an ice cream mixture that is being stirred by a stand mixer, liquid nitrogen quickly freezes it into ice cream. Understandably, though, the extreme temperature makes this more dangerous to work with.

A final option from more than two hundred years ago is to use a big bag of ice, crushed into small chunks mixed with a generous amount of salt. The salt lowers the melting point of the ice, so you end up with ex-

tremely cold, salty water. Place the ice cream mixture into a metal container and put the container in the center of the icy water. Scrape down the sides of the bowl and stir regularly. This will not make ice cream with as soft or airy a texture as some made with a machine, but is a fun experiment.

FAT

The fat from the cream, milk, and egg yolks gives ice cream its velvety, creamy mouthfeel. It does this by helping to stabilize the air bubbles and keep them small.

AIR

The main role of air in ice cream is to make it softer. Interestingly, because ice cream is sold by volume, not weight, air is also a good moneymaker for commercial ice creameries. Cheaper ice creams will be up to 50 percent air, while premium brands will have only around 30 percent air and will therefore taste more dense and creamy.

At home, you can adjust the air content by changing the speed at which you churn your mixture. Typically, the faster the churning blade turns, the more air you are adding.

SUGAR

As well as sweetening the ice cream, sugars also lower the freezing point of the mixture, which helps keep it softer when frozen. If you taste the ice cream base before it is frozen, it will seem very sweet, but once it comes out of your freezer, it will taste good. This is because our taste buds do not function as well when food is very cold.

fat

sugar

air bubbles

ice crystals

non-fat solids

OTHER SOLIDS

Milk and cream contain other nonfat solids like proteins. Egg yolks act as an emulsifier, which is important in ice cream to keep the fat and the water mixed together instead of separating into two layers. Commercial ice cream also has other additives to help stabilize the ice cream by keeping the ice crystals and air bubbles small while it is stored in freezers for a long time. These additives can be hard to acquire for home bakers and are not essential for making dreamy ice cream that is going to be eaten shortly after making.

COOKIES AND CREAM ICE CREAM

Who wouldn't love chewy chunks of chocolate chip cookie dough in every mouthful of creamy, homemade vanilla ice cream? Try it in a cone or in a deluxe sundae topped with whipped cream and chocolate sauce (page 142). Or try partnering it with piping hot apple turnovers (page 22).

Makes 1 quart (1 litre) of ice cream.

COOKIE DOUGH

½ cup (125 g / 4.4 oz) sugar
3 tablespoons (45 mL / 1.5 fl oz) water
¼ cup (50 g / 1.8 oz) butter
4 teaspoons (20 mL / 0.7 fl oz) milk
1 cup (160 g / 5.6 oz) plain or
    all-purpose flour
12.4 oz (350 g) mini chocolate chips

ICE CREAM

6 egg yolks (90 g / 3.2 oz)
1 cup (200 g / 7 oz) sugar
1½ cups (400 mL / 13.5 fl oz) milk
¾ cup (200 mL / 6.8 fl oz) heavy
    cream (35 percent fat)
seeds scraped from 1 vanilla bean
    or 2 teaspoons vanilla extract

COOKIE DOUGH

Heat the sugar and water in a saucepan until the sugar dissolves. Add the butter and milk. Once the butter is melted, add the flour. Stir over the heat for five minutes. This process causes the starch granules in the flour to burst, which makes the dough thicken and gets rid of any floury taste.

Spread your mixture onto a metal baking sheet and allow it to cool for 20 minutes. Mix through the chocolate chips.

ICE CREAM

Place the egg yolks and sugar into a bowl and whisk them together until they are pale in color. Pour the milk and cream into a saucepan and place over high heat until it just starts to boil, keeping an eye on it so that it does not bubble over. Remove from the heat, then add about a quarter of a cup of your hot cream mixture into the egg yolks and whisk well. Pour in the remainder of the hot cream, whisking as you do so. Add the vanilla extract. Return all of the mixture into the pan, add a candy thermometer, and stir over high heat until it reaches 85°C or 185°F. If you don't have a candy thermometer, you can set a timer and stir over high heat for 2 minutes, but keep a close eye on it as overheating this mixture will make it curdle. Pour through a fine sieve into a heatproof bowl, cover, and place into the fridge to chill for at least 3 hours.

Pour into an ice cream machine to freeze and churn for around 30 minutes or the time specified by your machine (see the chapter introduction for alternative churning methods). Add chunks of cookie dough to the ice cream, then pour the thick, cold mixture into a 1 L container and place in the freezer for a couple of hours to firm up.

ROASTED STRAWBERRY ICE CREAM

Do you ever find yourself peering through the glass at the ice cream shop wishing you could have a little taste of everything? I have, of course, tasted and enjoyed all of the ice creams in this chapter, and roasted strawberry is my favorite.

Makes 1 quart (1 litre) of ice cream.

ICE CREAM
3 ⅓ cups (500 g / 17.6 oz) fresh
    strawberries
¼ cup (55 g / 2 oz) sugar
¾ cup (200 mL / 6.8 fl oz) milk
6 large egg yolks (90 g / 3.2 oz)
¾ cup (160 g / 5.6 oz) caster sugar or
    superfine sugar
⅓ cup (100 mL / 3.4 fl oz) heavy
    cream (35 percent fat)

Preheat the oven to 165°C (325°F).

Wash the strawberries, hull them, and cut them in half lengthwise. Place them cut side down on a baking sheet covered with nonstick baking paper and sprinkle each one with sugar. Bake in the oven for 12-15 minutes or until the sugar is melted and the strawberries are soft.

Place the egg yolks and sugar into a bowl and whisk them together until they are pale in color. Pour the milk and cream into a saucepan and place over high heat until it just starts to boil. Keep an eye on it so that it does not boil over. Remove from the heat, add about a quarter of a cup of the hot cream mixture into the egg yolks, and whisk well. Pour in the remainder of the hot cream mixture, whisking as you pour. Return all of the mixture to the pan, add a candy thermometer, and stir over high heat until it reaches 85°C or 185°F. If you don't have a candy thermometer, set a timer and stir over high heat for 2 minutes, but watch carefully as overheating this mixture will make it curdle.

Remove from the heat and pour into a blender or food processor. Add the strawberries and any juice that is on the baking sheet, then process until smooth. (If you don't have a blender, push the mixture through a sieve using the back of a spoon.) Strain through a fine sieve to remove the seeds, cover, and put in the fridge to chill for at least 3 hours.

Freeze and churn the mixture using an ice cream machine for around 30 minutes (or the time specified by your appliance). See the chapter introduction for alternative churning methods.

Pour into a container and return to the freezer for a few hours to firm up.

Video tutorial for this recipe can be found at howtocookthat.net/cookbook

DARK CHOCOLATE GELATO (EGG FREE)

Chocolate gelato is always a crowd-pleaser. It can be dressed up in a sundae or eaten by itself. Try it with fresh strawberries and warm chocolate sauce (page 142) or drizzled with caramel (page 62).

Makes ⅓ gallon (1.5 litres).

CHOCOLATE GELATO

3.5 oz (100 g) dark chocolate

½ cups (150 mL / 5.1 fl oz) heavy cream (35 percent fat)

¾ cups (180 g / 6.4 oz) caster sugar or superfine sugar

⅓ cup (50 g / 1.8 oz) skim milk powder

½ cup (60 g / 2.1 oz) cocoa powder

2 ⅓ cups (600 mL / 20.3 fl oz) milk

Pour the cream and chocolate into a bowl and microwave on high for 30 seconds, then stir, heat 30 seconds more and stir again, then repeat in 10-second bursts, stirring each time, until there are no lumps of unmelted chocolate remaining. Whisk to combine the cream and chocolate, then set it aside.

Combine the sugar, cocoa powder, and skim milk in a bowl, then add enough milk to make the mixture wet. If you rub it between your fingers, this mixture will feel gritty because of the sugar. Heat it in the microwave for 60 seconds on high, stir, then repeat in 20-second bursts, stirring after each time, until the sugar is dissolved. Whisk your cream mixture into the chocolate. Add the milk and whisk until it is well combined. Cover and refrigerate for at least 3 hours or until completely chilled.

Pour your mixture into an ice cream machine to freeze and churn for around 30 minutes (or the time specified by your machine). See the chapter introduction for alternative churning methods.

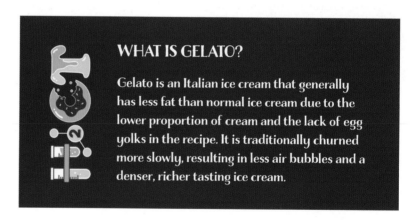

WHAT IS GELATO?

Gelato is an Italian ice cream that generally has less fat than normal ice cream due to the lower proportion of cream and the lack of egg yolks in the recipe. It is traditionally churned more slowly, resulting in less air bubbles and a denser, richer tasting ice cream.

Video tutorial for this recipe can be found at howtocookthat.net/cookbook

MATCHA GREEN TEA ICE CREAM

Calling all tea lovers, this is the ice cream for you. You can swap out the matcha green tea for any flavor tea that you prefer. While this recipe makes quite a strong matcha tea ice cream, you can simply reduce the number of tea bags for a subtler flavor.

Makes 1 quart (1 litre).

ICE CREAM
16 matcha green tea bags

1 ¼ cup (300 mL / 10 fl oz) boiling water

6 egg yolks (90 g / 3.2 oz)

1 cup (215 g / 7.6 oz) caster sugar or superfine sugar

¾ cup (200 mL / 6.8 fl oz) milk

⅓ cup (100 mL / 3.4 fl oz) heavy cream (35 percent fat)

2 drops green gel food coloring (optional)

Hang the teabags on the side of a heatproof jug. Add the boiling water to the jug and leave them to infuse for 5 minutes. Remove the teabags, squeezing as much liquid and flavor out of each one as possible.

Place the egg yolks and sugar in a bowl and whisk them together until they are pale in color. Pour the milk and cream into a saucepan, then place over high heat until it just starts to boil. Keep an eye on it so it doesn't boil over. Remove from the heat, add about a quarter of a cup of the hot cream mixture into the egg yolks, and whisk well. Return into the pan, whisking as you do so. Add a candy thermometer and stir over high heat until it reaches 85°C or 185°F. If you don't have a candy thermometer, set a timer and stir over high heat for 2 minutes only (overheating this mixture will make it curdle). Remove from the heat, add your tea and some green food coloring if desired, and then pour the liquid through a fine sieve into a heatproof bowl. Cover and place in the fridge to chill for at least 3 hours.

Place into an ice cream machine to freeze and churn for around 30 minutes (or the time specified by your appliance). See the chapter introduction for alternative churning methods. Pour into a 1 L container and place into the freezer for a couple of hours to firm up.

Video tutorial for this recipe can be found at howtocookthat.net/cookbook

STARBURST CHERRY ICE CREAM

This is a creamy ice cream with a full-on Starburst cherry flavor punch! If cherry Starburst doesn't particularly ring your bell, you can swap them out for your favorite chewy candy.

Makes 1 quart (1 litre) of ice cream.

ICE CREAM

1 ⅓ cups (200 g / 7 oz) Starburst cherry candies

1 ½ cups (400 mL / 13.5 fl oz) milk

⅓ cup (100 mL / 3.4 fl oz) heavy cream (35 percent fat)

6 egg yolks (90 g / 3.2 oz)

¼ cup (54 g / 2 oz) caster sugar or superfine sugar

Slice four of the Starburst candies into small pieces and set aside for later. You can use any flavor Starburst or a combination of two so long as they have a similar color, such as strawberry and cherry candies. Put the remaining Starburst candies into a saucepan with the milk and cream. Stir over high heat until they are dissolved, then remove from the heat.

In a separate bowl, whisk together the sugar and egg yolks until pale in color. Whisk in the Starburst mixture a little at a time. Pour it back into the saucepan, add a candy thermometer, and stir over high heat until it reaches 85°C (185°F). If you don't have a candy thermometer, you can set a timer and stir over high heat for 2 minutes only—note that overheating this mixture will make it curdle and go lumpy. Remove from the heat and pour it through a fine sieve into a heatproof bowl. Cover and place in the fridge to chill for at least 3 hours.

Place into an ice cream machine to freeze and churn for around 30 minutes (or the time specified by your appliance). See the chapter introduction for alternative churning methods.

Stir through the chopped Starburst candies, then pour the ice cream into a 1 L container and place into the freezer for a couple of hours to firm up.

Video tutorial for this recipe can be found at howtocookthat.net/cookbook

EASY NUTELLA SOFT SERVE

This is an easy fruit-based treat for when the kids get home from school. The frozen bananas make this soft serve thick, and the Nutella provides the sweetness and subtle chocolate flavor.

Makes 4 cones
(700 mL / 24 fl oz)
of soft serve.

SOFT SERVE
4 bananas (480 g / 17 oz)

3 tablespoons (25 g / 0.9 oz) Nutella

4 ice cream cones

Line an airtight container with baking paper. Peel and slice your bananas into the container and freeze overnight.

Place the Nutella and frozen bananas into a food processor and blend until the mixture is smooth and thick. For that classic soft serve ice cream look, pipe into ice cream cones using a star-shaped nozzle and serve immediately.

Video tutorial for this recipe can be found at howtocookthat.net/cookbook

GIANT ICE CREAM SANDWICH

I can still remember the gasps of excitement from children and parents alike when I brought this Giant Ice Cream Sandwich to the table for my son's seventh birthday party. Cake can be hit-or-miss with little party guests, but ice cream is always a winner!

Makes 75 portions, each serving equivalent to one scoop of ice cream and two normal cookies. However, if this is the only dessert at the party then expect it to serve around 50 as most people will ask for seconds.

CHOCOLATE CHIPS
25 oz (700 g) compound milk chocolate

COOKIES
(makes two very large cookies)
4 cups (880 g / 31 oz) margarine or butter
4 cups (865 g / 30.5 oz) caster sugar or superfine sugar
4 cups (930 g / 32.8 oz) brown sugar, firmly packed
8 eggs (400 g / 14 oz)
2 tablespoons vanilla
12 cups (1920 g / 68 oz) plain or all-purpose flour
4 teaspoons baking powder

ICE CREAM
2½ gallons (9.5 litres) vanilla ice cream

EQUIPMENT
Giant-size chocolate chip mold (you can use either a giant Hershey kiss mold or a rounded funnel)
12-inch (31 cm) round cake pan
15-inch (38 cm) square or round cake board
14 x 16 inch (36 x 41 cm) metal baking sheet

CHOCOLATE CHIPS

Melt the chocolate in the microwave for 60 seconds on high, then stir, microwave 30 seconds and stir again, then repeat in bursts of 30 seconds, stirring after each until melted. Pour into the mold and set in the fridge. If you are using a funnel as a mold, you can seal the funnel tube with compacted aluminum foil, then place it into a cup to hold it upright. Repeat this process to make eight giant chocolate chips.

COOKIES

Firstly, check the size of your freezer to ensure that the cake board will fit. If not, scale down the size of the cookies and ice cream accordingly.

Preheat the oven to 150°C (300°F).

Using an electric mixer, mix together the butter and sugars until smooth (there is no need to whip). Add the vanilla and eggs and beat thoroughly. Mix in the flour and baking powder.

Cover two baking sheets with baking paper and split the dough between them. Flatten into two 11 inch (28 cm) circles. Put flour on your hands and shape each into a smooth round cookie. They will spread in the oven, so make sure there is adequate room on the baking sheet. Cut four of the chocolate chips in half. Put one whole chocolate chip and three chip halves onto each cookie.

Place an empty baking sheet on the very top shelf of the oven to protect the top of the cookie from getting over-browned. Bake the cookie in the middle of the oven for 60 minutes. Remove from oven and, while it is hot, arrange the extra pieces of chocolate chips, letting them melt slightly into the top. Allow to cool.

ICE CREAM

Line the base and sides of the cake pan or tin with baking paper, allowing the paper on the sides to stick out above the top rim of the pan. Fill the pan with vanilla ice cream, squashing it down to fill any gaps and to make it level on top.

Note: If you have scaled down the size of your ice cream sandwich, use a round cake pan that is slightly smaller than your cookie. To calculate how much ice cream you need to buy, measure the volume of your cake pan using a measuring jug and water, then multiply the results by 1.5. For example, the volume of my cake pan was 1.6 gallons (6 litres) so I multiplied that by 1.5 and purchased 2.4 gallons (9 litres) of ice cream.

ASSEMBLY

Choose the cookie that you like the best, and set that one aside for the top of the ice cream sandwich. Now take the other cookie and cut the tops off the chocolate chips so the cookie will sit flat. Put a board on top of it and flip it over.

Take the ice cream out of the freezer and loosen it from the cake pan by pulling the baking paper on the sides. Tip it upside down and shake it until it falls out. Place the ice cream on top of the base cookie and peel away the baking paper.

Add the other cookie on top, then wrap the sandwich in plastic wrap and store in the freezer until ready to serve.

Video tutorial for this recipe can be found at howtocookthat.net/cookbook

Giant Ice Cream Sandwich

GIANT MAGNUM EGO

Is there any better way to celebrate a really big milestone in someone's life than by recreating a huge, 15 pound (7 kg), double chocolate-coated caramel Magnum Ego? The world's most popular ice cream is about to get supersized!

Serves 40 to 75 people, depending on how giant the servings are!

SOFT CARAMEL

2 cups (670 g / 23.6 oz) glucose syrup or light corn syrup

2 cups (500 mL / 17 fl oz) heavy cream (35 percent fat)

1 cup (250 mL / 8.4 fl oz) milk

3 cups (650 g / 23 oz) sugar

Additional 1 ⅔ cups (400 mL / 13.5 fl oz) heavy cream (35 percent fat)

14 oz (400 g) white chocolate

Brown, orange, and yellow food coloring

ICE CREAM AND CHOCOLATE COATING

2 ¾ gallons (10 litres) vanilla ice cream

4 pounds (1.8 kg) milk chocolate

2 bottles Ice Magic or Magic Shell chocolate topping

ICE CREAM STICK

21.2 oz (600 g) white chocolate

3 tablespoons unsweetened cocoa powder

EQUIPMENT

Ice cream template (see page 182), covered in clear contact paper

Two 12-inch (30 cm) cake-support sticks

Candy thermometer

2 boards, 26 x 11 inch (65 x 26 cm)

Brownie pan (or a large shallow pan) two thirds full of water, freeze to make a tray of ice

Acetate or thin bendy plastic

SOFT CARAMEL

Combine the glucose syrup, 2 cups of cream, milk, and sugar in a pan. Stir over high heat until the sugar dissolves. Continue to heat, stirring occasionally until it reaches 116°C (241°F), by which stage it will be thickened and a light golden-brown color.

Add the additional cream and stir until combined. Bring the mixture back up to 104°C (219°F). Remove from the heat and add in the white chocolate. Wait 60 seconds for it to melt, then whisk until smooth. Add food coloring to make it a deeper brown color if desired. Pour into a heatproof bowl and leave for several hours to cool and thicken.

ICE CREAM STICK

Heat your white chocolate in the microwave for 60 seconds on high, stir, and repeat in 30-second bursts, stirring each time until melted. Mix in 2 tablespoons of cocoa powder.

Place the template (see page 182) on the counter and cover in baking paper. Pour on half of the chocolate and cover the area of the ice cream stick. The stick needs to be quite thick, so allow it to flow a little beyond the size shown on the template. Lay the two cake-support sticks onto the chocolate so they run the length of the handle and stick out 10 cm (4 inches) beyond the flat end. Pour the rest of the white chocolate over the top to cover the sticks. Sprinkle with a little more cocoa powder, then spread gently with an offset spatula to flatten the top and slightly mix in the cocoa powder. Once it is starting to set, place the template on top and cut around the shape of the ice cream stick. Remove the template; then, using the tip of the knife, run down the stick in a wavy wood grain pattern. Place the chocolate stick in the fridge.

CONSTRUCTION

Place 1.3 pounds (600 g) of milk chocolate into a bowl, microwave for 60 seconds on high, and stir, then microwave 30 seconds and stir again. Continue with 30-second bursts followed by stirring until melted.

Place the template onto one of the boards and cover with a sheet of baking paper. Pour milk chocolate over the top and spread it out into a smooth layer just beyond the edge of the template. Pull the template out from underneath the baking paper. Once the chocolate starts to set, put the template on top and cut around it. Now set it aside.

Take your tubs of ice cream out of the freezer and cut slices the width of the "thickness guide" on the template. Put a piece of baking paper over the second board and line the ice cream chunks up next to each other.

Smooth out the surface using a spatula—it should be the height of the thickness guide. Place the ice cream template over the top and shape the ice cream, cutting off any areas that are sticking out and adding these offcuts into any gaps. If the ice cream gets too soft during this process, put it back into the freezer for an hour. Dialing the freezer down to its coldest setting will make this easier. Once it is the right shape, put it in the freezer.

Cover the chocolate piece with one third of the caramel, spreading it almost to the edges. Spread a thin even layer of Ice Magic (or Magic Shell) topping over the top. Put the ice tray under the board. Take the shaped ice cream out of the freezer. Line up the top of the ice cream with the top of the chocolate shape. Then begin to pull the baking paper around under the board so that the ice cream slowly slides off on top of the chocolate.

Pour a whole bottle of Ice Magic over the ice cream and spread it out quickly before it sets. Cover the sides of the ice cream in Ice Magic using a spatula. Place the ice cream and ice tray into the freezer for 1 hour.

Cover the top and sides with caramel, spreading it into a smooth even layer. Add the white chocolate ice cream stick by pushing the support sticks into the base of the Giant Magnum. The stick should be sitting in midair, halfway between the board and the top of the ice cream. Return to the freezer for at least one hour.

Melt the rest of your milk chocolate in the microwave. Cut a strip of acetate the height of the side of the ice cream and long enough to wrap halfway around it. Cover the acetate in a layer of melted milk chocolate. Once it is starting to set but is still soft, lift it up and quickly wrap it around one side of the ice cream. If any chocolate leaks out of the base, use a knife to trim it off. Repeat on the other side. Leave the acetate in place, then pour the remaining milk chocolate on top and spread it out—you'll need to move quickly because the ice cream is cold, so the chocolate will set fast.

Place your Giant Magnum in the freezer until you are ready to serve. Peel off the acetate and serve to the table with the tray of ice or dry ice pellets underneath it.

Video tutorial for this recipe can be found at howtocookthat.net/cookbook

Giant Magnum Ego

$1,000 ICE CREAM SUNDAE

If you have money to burn, you can head to Serendipity 3 in New York and order this amazing golden dessert for a cool $1,000. It's in **The Guinness Book of World Records** as the most expensive ice cream sundae on Earth! I had a blast recreating it using the same pricey ingredients as Serendipity. You can of course substitute cheaper ingredients, and it will still be delicious.

SUPER CREAMY ICE CREAM

Enough for 5 sundaes

2 Tahitian grade A gourmet vanilla beans

1⅔ cups (375 mL / 12.7 fl oz) heavy cream (35 percent fat)

1⅔ cups (375 mL / 12.7 fl oz) crème fraîche

1 cup (150 g / 5.3 oz) caster sugar or superfine sugar

8 egg yolks (120 g / 4.2 oz)

CHOCOLATE SAUCE

Enough for 2 sundaes

2.5 oz (70 g) Amedei Chuao Napolitains dark chocolate

¼ cup (65 mL / 2.2 fl oz) heavy cream (35 percent fat)

PRESENTATION

For each serving, you will need:

1 crystal goblet

1 gold spoon

3 squares Amedei Porcelana Napolitains dark chocolate

continued on next page

SUPER CREAMY ICE CREAM

Cut the vanilla bean in half lengthwise, then open it up to flatten it slightly and run a knife down the middle to collect all the seeds. Put the seeds and the pods into a pan with the cream and crème fraîche. Heat until it just starts to boil, watching that it does not bubble over. Take off the heat and set aside for 10 minutes for the vanilla flavor to infuse into the cream.

In a separate bowl, whisk together the sugar and egg yolks. Bring the cream mixture back up to the boil. While whisking, pour about ½ cup of the hot cream into your egg yolk mixture. Then add your warm egg yolk mixture back into the rest of the cream in the pan and whisk well to combine. Stir over high heat for about 60 seconds more, but do not overheat or the mixture will split and go lumpy. You'll know it is ready if you slightly tip the pan and the mixture is starting to form a thin layer on the base. Immediately remove from the heat and pour through a sieve into a heatproof bowl. Cover and refrigerate for at least 4 hours or until cold.

Place in an ice cream machine and churn for 20 minutes. Pour into an airtight container and put it in the freezer for at least 1 hour to harden.

CHOCOLATE SAUCE

Place the chocolate into a bowl. Heat the cream until it is nearly boiling. Pour the cream over the chocolate and leave for two minutes for the chocolate to melt. Stir together, mixing quickly until it forms a smooth chocolate ganache. Cover and leave at room temperature to cool.

AMEDEI CHUAO & PORCELANA

Just as there are different types of coffee beans, each with a unique flavor, there are also many varieties of cocoa beans (cacao). Amedei Chuao, the world's rarest chocolate, and Amedei Porcelana, the world's most expensive chocolate, are made from varieties of Venezuelan beans that are classed as having a fine cocoa flavor. These particular cocoa trees are low in yield and highly susceptible to pests and diseases. Because of this, they have been largely ripped out and replaced with better yielding varieties. This makes their beans very rare and expensive. You can substitute with a different brand of dark chocolate that has 80 percent cocoa or more.

7 gold sugarcoated almonds

5 sheets edible gold leaf

Candied fruits from Paris

1 Madagascan vanilla bean

1 spoonful of Grand Passion
    whitefish roe (dessert caviar)

2 chocolate truffles

Gum paste cattleya orchid sprayed
    with edible gold food coloring

ASSEMBLY

Place two sheets of edible gold into the goblet. Make sure you purchase 100 percent edible gold leaf from a reputable supplier as it is very important that it does not contain any traces of poisonous heavy metals such as lead or cadmium. Put three scoops of ice cream onto a cold plate, then scrape the seeds out of the Madagascan vanilla bean and dab some on top of the ice cream. Cover each scoop with a sheet of gold leaf.

Place one scoop of the gold-coated ice cream in the goblet and drizzle with a spoonful of chocolate sauce. Add the remaining two scoops of ice cream and another spoonful of sauce. Decorate with some candied fruits, gold-covered sugared almonds, and three squares of Amedei Porcelana chocolate. Add the sugar flower to the top of the dessert and serve with a few more sugared almonds and two chocolate truffles on the plate. If you happen to live in the USA, you can also top it with a small spoon of dessert caviar. This caviar cannot be shipped internationally as it must be kept refrigerated.

Video tutorial for this recipe can be found at howtocookthat.net/cookbook

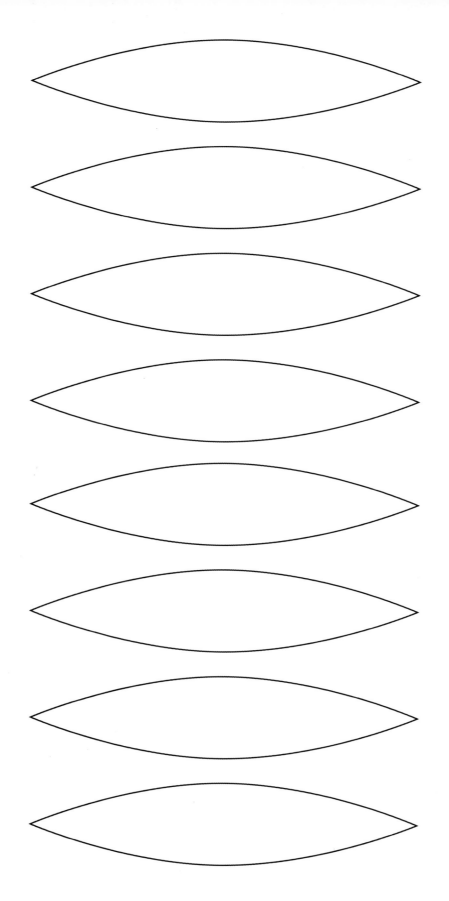

Chocolate Flower Petal Template, recipe on page 56

Macaron Template, recipe on page 132

— JOIN HERE 1 —

Giant Magnum Template, recipe on page 172

— JOIN HERE 1 —

— JOIN HERE 2 —

– JOIN HERE 2 –

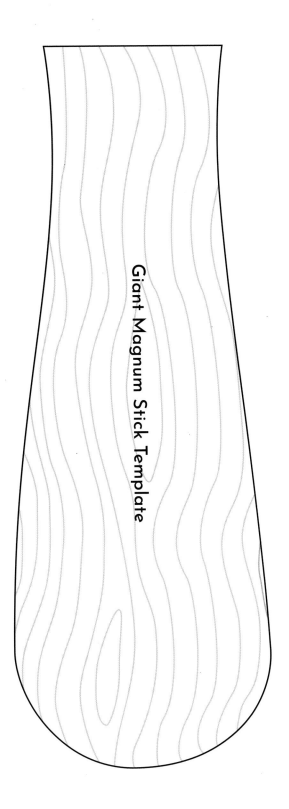

Giant Magnum Stick Template

Giant Magnum Height of Ice Cream

ACKNOWLEDGEMENTS

Thank you to my wonderful friends and family who have been with me on this journey and enjoyed all the crazy, sweet creations that I've dished up.

Thanks so much to my subscribers and patrons. Your feedback, requests, and encouragement over the years have pushed me beyond my limits and inspired me to invent new things. And yes, your requests for a cookbook have finally been heard!

To the talented Joanie Simon, thank you for your enthusiasm, organization, and amazing styling and food photography skills. I'm so happy with how it has turned out. We should do this again some time.

To Lance Whipple, what a privilege it has been to have someone as experienced as you working behind the scenes to help remake my creations ready for photography.

To my lovely sister, thanks for your enthusiasm, encouragement, and advice throughout this project.

Thanks to the whole team at Mango for your expertise in the competitive world of publishing. To Brenda Knight, Chris McKenney and Debbie Hartung, thanks for being such a pleasure to work with throughout the process of writing this book, from concept to delivery. Morgane Leoni, thanks for all your hard work on layout and design, it looks brilliant.

To the late, great Hannah Glasse, thanks for taking the time to write out recipes in *The Compleat Confectioner* 260 years ago. Your wonderful book is one of the many old cookbooks that inspired me to write down my own recipes for future generations.

Very special love and appreciation to my husband Dave for always believing in whatever crazy projects I undertake. Thanks for all your support, for being my best friend, and of course your journalistic editing and wordsmith skills.

And finally to my three boys, James, Matthew, and Jedd, for being patient when I'm working and for always being willing to taste test and give genuine opinions on endless baking experiments. I love you to the moon and back.

ABOUT THE AUTHOR

Ann Reardon is a wildly inventive food scientist, dietician, and pastry chef whose crazy, sweet creations draw millions of fans each week all around the world. Episodes of Ann's award-winning series *How to Cook That* have been viewed almost a billion times by foodies and cooking enthusiasts, all eager to learn the secrets to her extravagant cakes, chocolate, and desserts. As well as producing a nonstop carnival of eye-popping creations and fun baking challenges, Ann is also a gifted teacher who gives clear, no-nonsense instructions for people to recreate her recipes as their own masterpieces at home. She was voted the world's best online chef in the US Taste Awards, and her culinary artistry has been celebrated on a myriad of TV programs and websites as well as in newspapers.

Interestingly, Ann wasn't someone who ever sought the spotlight. After graduating with a bachelor's degree in food science and postgraduate in dietetics, she worked as a community dietician and then a youth counselor before eventually heading online to launch the How to Cook That website and YouTube channel a decade ago. Ann also designed the world's first 3D augmented reality baking app, a zany invention that topped the download charts in twenty-five countries. She lives in Melbourne, Australia, with her husband Dave and their three handsome boys. who regularly appear on the show—and thoroughly enjoy sampling her delicious creations!

HOWTOCOOKTHAT.NET
YOUTUBE.COM/HOWTOCOOKTHAT
FACEBOOK.COM/HOWTOCOOKTHAT

BAKING EQUIPMENT

ESSENTIAL

Measuring Spoons

A set of measuring spoons will be used more often than you imagine. While a teaspoon measure is the same around the world, tablespoons vary between countries. In this book, 1 tablespoon is equal to 15 mL (0.5 fl oz) or 3 teaspoons.

Baking Pans (Tins)

The most common baking pans used in my kitchen are round 20 cm (8 inch) pans, rectangular 25 x 38 cm (10 x 15 inch) brownie or slice pans, a cupcake pan, and a flat baking sheet.

Rolling Pin

Rolling pins are generally not expensive, but if you don't have one, you can always use a bottle with straight sides. However, the handles on a rolling pin make the job easier.

Cooling Rack

Air needs to circulate around freshly baked cakes and cookies as they cool to ensure that condensation doesn't form underneath, resulting in a soggy bottom.

Rubber Spatulas

As well as being the perfect tool for scraping a bowl clean, rubber spatulas are undoubtedly the best choice for folding ingredients together.

Sieve

Fine and coarse metal sieves are basic tools in the kitchen. They are used for aerating dry ingredients and making smooth purees by pressing wet ingredients through them.

Whisk

A whisk is superior to a spoon when it comes to combining ingredients like cream and melted chocolate.

Electric Hand Mixer

While you could use a whisk to whip cream or egg whites, an electric hand mixer will save you a lot of time and effort.

Scales

Digital scales that can be adjusted with a tare weight to read zero are a must-have in any baker's kitchen. While cup measurements are provided in this book, scales are definitely the most accurate way to measure ingredients. Measuring cups vary in size around the world; in this book, a 250 mL (8.45 fl oz) cup has been used. And, of course, how tightly ingredients are packed into the cup changes the quantity. On top of that, weighed recipe amounts are often rounded up or down to the closest cup measure. All of these factors can add up to a big difference in the finished recipe.

Candy Thermometer

I recommend finding a digital candy thermometer that can clip onto the side of a pan. You will need a thermometer for tempering chocolate, heating cream and egg yolks without curdling them, and measuring the temperature of sugar solutions when making Italian meringue, candy, and caramel.

NICE TO HAVE

Ice Cream Scoops

A scoop with a spring-loaded handle to release the ice cream can also be handy in the kitchen for portioning and cleanly delivering an even amount of cake mixture into each cup in cupcake pans.

Offset Spatula

An offset spatula is pleasant to hold and makes the job of spreading cream and frosting onto cakes a little easier.

Blender

A blender makes quick work of crumbling cookies, pureeing wet ingredients, and making yummy milkshakes.

Stand Mixer

Every baker's dream is to own a lovely stand mixer. The good news is that you can actually make everything in this book using just a hand mixer, so there is no need to splurge...unless you need an excuse to buy one—then go ahead.

INDEX

Published by Mango Publishing Group, a division of Mango Media Inc.

Cover & Food Photography: © Joanie Simon
Cover, Layout & Design: Morgane Leoni

For permission requests, please contact the publisher at:

Mango Publishing Group
2850 S Douglas Road, 2nd Floor
Coral Gables, FL 33134 USA
info@mango.bz

For special orders, quantity sales, course adoptions and corporate sales, please
email the publisher at sales@mango.bz. For trade and wholesale sales, please
contact Ingram Publisher Services at customer.service@ingramcontent.com or
+1.800.509.4887.

How to Cook That: Crazy Sweet Creations

Library of Congress Cataloging-in-Publication number: 2021934482
ISBN: (print) 978-1-64250-578-8, (ebook) 978-1-64250-579-5
BISAC Category Code CKB024000, COOKING / Courses & Dishes / Desserts

Printed in the United States of America